OWN IT.

OWN IT.

MAKE YOUR
ANXIETY
WORK FOR YOU

CAROLINE FORAN

THE EXPERIMENT

NEW YORK

The Experiment, LLC, 220 East 23rd Street, Suite 600, New York, NY 10010-4658
theexperimentpublishing.com

Library of Congress Cataloging-in-Publication Data

Names: Foran, Caroline, author.
Title: Own it : make your anxiety work for you / Caroline Foran.
Other titles: Owning it
Description: New York : The Experiment, 2019. | "Originally published in
  Ireland as Owning It by Hachette Books Ireland in 2017." | Includes
  bibliographical references.
Identifiers: LCCN 2018054470 (print) | LCCN 2018057911 (ebook) | ISBN
  9781615195626 (ebook) | ISBN 9781615195619 (pbk.)
Subjects: LCSH: Anxiety. | Fear. | Self-help techniques.
Classification: LCC BF575.A6 (ebook) | LCC BF575.A6 F67 2019 (print) | DDC
  152.4/6--dc23
LC record available at https://lccn.loc.gov/2018054470

ISBN 978-1-61519-561-9
Ebook ISBN 978-1-61519-562-6

Cover design by Sarah Smith and Beth Bugler | Text design by Beth Bugler
Author photograph by Nathalie Marquez Courtney

Manufactured in the United States of America

First printing April 2019
10 9 8 7 6 5 4 3 2 1

For my main squeeze

Contents

Introduction: What this book will do for you

This whole idea of "curing" your anxiety so that you never have to feel it again—which plenty of books out there claim to do, preying on your vulnerability—only serves to make you feel worse in the long run.

DISCLAIMER 1: The first and perhaps most important point you can take from the following 250 or so pages is that I am not in any way, shape or form a healthcare professional. I don't have a degree in psychology or any qualifications that would otherwise allow me to make specific recommendations to you on how to deal with the veritable sh*t show that is your current experience of anxiety.

However, now that you've bothered to pick up this book, here's what I *can* offer: experience and empathy (as well as a whole lotta research).

DISCLAIMER 2: The truth is, this book won't "cure" your anxiety. I'm sorry; you probably hated reading that; you just want to feel better (like yesterday) and I understand that, I did, too. But here's something you might not have heard before; this whole idea of "curing" your anxiety so that you never have to feel it again—which plenty of books out there claim to do, preying on your vulnerability—only serves to make you feel worse in the long run. Watch out for that: I wasted a small fortune chasing these very same quick fixes and sensationalist claims.

What you *will* get from this book is the understanding voice of someone who's felt as crap as you do now and, like you, has no time for BS or overly technical jargon that makes everything sound a whole lot scarier than it needs to be. Anxiety, by its very nature, is disconcerting enough; this book aims to keep things simple and break down what anxiety is so that you can regain control.

The main aim of this book—and what I want to get you thinking about before we dive right in—is the idea of OWNING your anxiety so that it no longer negatively impacts your life.

This book is about changing your relationship with your anxiety. Though your instincts right now are telling you otherwise, the key is not to resist it. Not to run a million miles away from it. Not to cure it. But to learn the art of managing it.

OWN IT.

Anxiety is something we will all encounter at some point in our lives; some of us just feel it more than others. As for those whom you look at enviously, wondering how they go through life so seemingly carefree, perhaps it will be just a matter of time before anxiety rears its ugly head for them too—or maybe they're already feeling it on the inside and you just don't know it.

You see, there's no stereotypical or easily identifiable anxiety sufferer. We don't walk around breathing erratically into brown paper bags or set our Facebook status to "anxious" for all the world to see. Though it's far from the upbeat perspective you're looking for, stress and anxiety are nearly impossible to avoid in the twenty-first century, and the last thing I want to do is tell you how to live a stress-free and anxiety-free life. I tried that, as many have, but it doesn't work; it's futile. You just end up feeling frustrated and more anxious, and all that improves is your self-help book collection.

Thankfully, though, what *is* possible is managing anxiety and, better still, making it work for you, whatever your age.

Throughout *Own It*, I will chronicle my own experience of anxiety—a lot of which you'll no doubt recognize in yourself—and I will share the most practical and positive tools that can help you feel like you again. When you're right in the thick of it or plummeting deep down into the abyss, which is how a bad bout of anxiety can feel, it's hard to imagine that there'll ever be a time when you won't feel untethered or unable to cope. My aim here is to reassure you that you will. You'll fly it.

So, you're probably wondering, now that I no longer feel defined by my anxiety—or the need to introduce myself with a warning, like: "Hello, I'm an anxious person and I might, at any moment, burst into flames"—why would I want to drag it all up again? Why don't I just go on living my life to the fullest without giving too much oxygen to a bad experience? The thing is, I know for sure that my own anxiety wouldn't have been anywhere near as traumatic if I had known then what I know now. And with so many people starting to come out of the woodwork and admit that they, too, don't feel so good, I want to share my learnings—good and bad—so that you can also pull yourself out of that initial black hole of despair and learn to cope. Most importantly, though, I want to be honest and to the point, as I believe this will save you time, money and any further, unnecessary suffering.

You see, when my anxiety hit me like a big fat freight train that I just did not see coming, I was desperate to talk to someone who *wasn't* a professional. For me, "professionals" were people who were incredibly well read and qualified on the subject, but who lacked any real empathetic insight into just how sh*tty I was feeling. When I felt like my world had come crashing down for no good reason, I wanted to see proof of a real, live, functioning human being who'd felt like I had and lived to tell the tale. That's all the comfort and reassurance I needed; to know that when my parents or a professional said, "There's always a light at the end of the tunnel," that I could see, firsthand, that this was true and not just something they were saying to comfort me.

The final thing to consider, before getting down to business, is a sentiment (call it a mantra or an affirmation if you will) that I want you to get comfortable with saying. Repeat it now, five times, out loud (you're going to have to get very used to reaffirming yourself, so let's jump straight in): "It's okay that I don't feel okay. I will be okay soon. I'm going to get through this and I will never have to go through this experience again." It's important to note that even though you don't feel okay, you are still very much together underneath it all.

I say that you'll never have to go through this again because it's true, and not because it sounds like something contrived that you'll find on Pinterest with a swirly font. It's very hard to convince yourself of this when you feel like you're all but losing your mind, but get familiar with this idea now. Someday soon, you'll wish you could go back in time and reassure yourself of this inevitability. Sometimes, even now (because I'm still human), I think: "My anxiety took me completely off guard before, and I fell apart, who's to say that won't happen again?" And then I stop myself: I will never, not for the rest of my life, be taken by surprise by anxiety and fall entirely victim to its power.

Today, I know too much. I understand it entirely. I now accept that I'm a sensitive creature who feels things a little more than the person next to me might, and I'm okay with that.

I recognize the signs and the symptoms of anxiety; I know how to manage them; and, not only am I able to put out fires as they arise, I can prevent the fires from arising by taking really good care of myself.

Though I've got a good handle on it (well you'd certainly hope so, now that you've bought this book), I don't consider myself to be particularly enlightened. I did not, unfortunately, have an *Eat Pray Love* kind of epiphany. I did not go to Bali and meet an all-seeing, toothless medicine man who schooled me in the art of living in the here and now (but hey, that might help) and I'm still not particularly good at meditation. I still have sh*tty, stressful work days, or days when I feel a little below par—one day when I was particularly exhausted, ratty and hormonal, I cried because my boyfriend ate my last chicken nugget—but that, dear reader, is the human experience, whether you're eighteen, twenty-eight or sixty-eight. What I have now, however, is a quiet confidence in myself to pull through the speed bumps and curveballs that life is sure to throw, thanks to the arsenal of effective tools that I keep tucked under my imaginary yellow umbrella. No matter how big the raincloud, I know now that it will pass. But there was a long time where I was never sure if it would.

So, let's talk about what this book can do for you. Rather than give you one giant mountain of reading to dive into—the prospect of which might just be enough to give you anxiety—this book is structured in two very simple parts that mirror how I strongly suggest you approach your own situation. For me, it's a tried-and-tested technique that I return to anytime I feel even the slightest bit wobbly. Even if you're feeling particularly woeful, just knowing that you've got a plan of action will give you the reassurance that all is not lost. So, let's get to it.

Assess (Or as I like to call it, What-the-f*ck-is-going-on?)

Beyond your own set of circumstances, you first need to understand what anxiety is, how it functions, why we feel it, why so many of us experience it, and why the presence of stress or anxiety in our bodies is actually nothing to worry about. You also need to wrap your head around something known as the "negativity bias." At first, it might seem like there's an awful lot of information to absorb, but don't be overwhelmed. This is a good thing; it means there are several ways through the fog and you're not destined for a life defined by anxiety. Take comfort in that.

Lest we forget, knowledge is power. Having a firm grasp of exactly what anxiety is and precisely why you're feeling it is half the battle. It really is. Most of my own suffering was born from not having the faintest clue about what was going on, an unwillingness to address why I was feeling it (out of fear, naturally) and just totally panicking about the fact that I was panicking, which, as you can imagine, was a fairly self-perpetuating quandary.

Before you throw the kitchen sink at your anxiety or trawl the internet in a blind panic for that one quick fix upon which you so desperately hope to stumble (please, resist the urge), you have to take stock of your current situation and the events that have led you here. What's going on?

Did it really come out of the blue? How long have you been feeling this way? What's happening in your life, e.g., relationships, exams at school, pressure at work? Now I'm not suggesting you answer each of these questions right here this second, otherwise the first part of this book would be rendered unnecessary. Together, we'll paint a clear picture.

Address (Or, What-the-f*ck-am-I-going-to-do-about-it?)

When you've done the work of part one, and successfully assessed your situation, we will move swiftly on to the art of addressing it.

The first time you educate yourself about anxiety is always the toughest because it's when you tend to feel the worst and the most overwhelmed. But when you've got a general understanding of it, it's then a matter of assessing individual bouts of anxiety as they arise. Eventually you'll get really good at saying, "Oh yes, I can see why I feel this way, that makes total sense," before employing the specific anti-anxiety tools that you know will work for you.

Within this section of the book, with the help of some incredibly qualified experts, we'll explore everything from what you put into your body to the many treatment options and tools that are available to you. Instead of attacking your anxiety like the enemy, we'll work with it, dealing with both the physical and the emotional symptoms so you, too, can Own It.

Throughout the book, you will also find a wealth of practical exercises to get unstuck, all of which were a huge help to me (and still are). Some of these exercises have been formulated with the help of Dr. Malie Coyne, clinical psychologist, while others are tried-and-tested favorites from some of the most helpful online resources.

My advice to you, before you go any further, is to pick up a journal of some sort, so that you can get to work with the exercises as you read.

Putting pen to paper will make a huge difference; you'll feel instantly empowered for having taken over the reins of your anxiety and you'll find it far easier to keep track of and notice your progress. If this feels futile at first—it did for me—keep at it. I promise it will help.

Between Parts 1 and 2, you'll find a series of quick and easy chapters that you can jump to any time you feel the need. These include my ultimate panic attack rescue guide, which will walk you through those particularly hairy moments; fifteen easy things you can do for your anxiety today; my anxiety survival kit; and plenty more.

On the whole, I've structured this book in such a way so you can dip in and out as you please; it doesn't have to be devoured in one go from cover to cover—and you can (and should!) return to the chapters that resonate most with you as often as you can. Keep it handy, throw it in your bag when you're on the go, and consider it your ultimate go-to whether you're feeling a little overwhelmed, you're right in the grip of a petrifying panic attack or whether you've been suffering below the surface for quite some time. Wherever you find yourself on the spectrum from carefree to anxious mess (I was certainly closer to the latter), you will find something within these pages that speaks to you.

Are you ready to Own It?

PART ONE

Assessing Anxiety

What is anxiety?

WHAT IS ANXIETY? A sh*t, scary feeling where—how do I put this?—you feel as though you're quite literally coming out of your own skin. Yep, that's it.

Granted, this chapter may have started like one of those state-the-obvious kind of chapters that you'd expect to find in a mental-health-for-dummies book. But it simply cannot be skipped, and there's a lot to take in. Understanding what anxiety is, why we have it and how it affects us is the first port of call on your journey toward wellness, and trust me, just having this knowledge alone can alleviate some of what you're feeling.

So, "anxiety" is a word you're well familiar with. It's a concept that's thrown about and overused on a daily basis, especially in today's exaggerated world of social media, where Harry Styles might fancy himself a haircut, leaving the rest of us unable to "cope" with the transformation. Though anxiety is something that we all seem to grasp, albeit loosely, few of us are versed in the specific brain chemistry that gives rise to feelings of anxiety. What's more, few of us succeed in identifying its presence within ourselves—I certainly did not.

I understood this basic bodily function in the sense that you might pace the floor "anxiously" awaiting the arrival of your exam results, or when, right before speaking in public, you'd pray the ground would open up and swallow you whole (that one still gets me).

I also had a vague understanding of the "fight-or-flight" response and how, at least from an evolutionary perspective, it was essential for our survival. It is our body's innate way of protecting itself and when you take a moment to think about it, it's actually kind of impressive. Obviously, it isn't a feeling you'd relish, but that kind of anxiety made sense. It was fleeting. It spurred you on. It showed that you cared. There was always an easily isolated reason that triggered it, and, like clockwork, it passed with the event.

Until, one day, with no big anxiety-inducing event around the corner and no life-threatening grizzly bears in my immediate vicinity, the very unsettling feeling of anxiety was just there.

Always. What I had absolutely no clue about was how stress and anxiety can manifest themselves in different ways. That near-constant ache in my stomach wasn't just because I had a dodgy tummy; it was because I was anxious, and that's how my body tried to communicate this information to me.

This kind of anxiety—the one that creeps up on you in the absence of any life-altering event—is more of a slow burner, and it can be really hard to identify. I drove myself insane trying to figure out why my stomach was so reactive. One minute, I'd convinced myself I was allergic to tap water; the next, I had every kind of cancer imaginable (because the internet told me so and I believed it). I wasn't thinking clearly, and was therefore incapable of rationally connecting the dots.

I wasn't listening to my body, and while my stomach certainly had my attention (it was just short of investing in a ouija board to spell it out for me), I wasn't looking at the full picture of my lifestyle, past and present, that may have been a contributing factor. Unbeknownst to my conscious mind, I was stressed out. Not the kind of tangible, I-have-to-get-through-this-to-do-list-right-now stress, but a deeper, quieter stress that erodes your ability to keep your sh*t together.

I ignored it—blaming the tap water was among the ridiculous conclusions I came to—and eventually my body cranked it up a notch. What started as subtle symptoms of stress eventually graduated to full-blown, I-can't-cope anxiety, otherwise defined as an intense negative emotion dominated by fear. And when I say

I couldn't cope, I mean that as literally as those words were originally intended to be understood (as opposed to when we "can't cope" with our celeb crush's tabloid headline).

The prolonged stress resulted in me developing an oversensitive nervous system, which made me more susceptible to external and internal stressors, irrational thoughts, worries and fear (all of which are defining characteristics of anxiety), and, in turn, this made me fearful of the fear itself. I was no longer flourishing or thriving; I wasn't sailing along. I was struggling to cope—literally—with the most basic aspects of living. And that, as you may know, is f*cking terrifying.

What was almost worse—and I appreciate how stupid this must sound, but bear with me—was the lack of dreadful things on which to pin the blame. Yes, I was experiencing prolonged stress, but I still had a roof over my head, food on the table, every conceivable convenience at my fingertips and all the support I could want. There was no trauma, nobody had died, I had no near-death experience that left me reeling and there was nothing remotely sinister in my midst. I'd even taken it upon myself not to watch another horror movie, in case it induced any disconcerting feelings.

On paper, my life seemed to be firing on all cylinders. I had no concerning health conditions; my family is only dysfunctional in the sense that all families are a little bit dysfunctional; I have a handful of brilliant friends; and I had just started a promising new media job with plenty of potential. Career-wise, I was doing better than I could have hoped for in my mid-twenties. After a picture-perfect trip to New York, my boyfriend and I (nauseatingly in love) decided to move into a gorgeous apartment in Dublin, ticking the personal life boxes nicely, too. Aside from the occasional spot breakout, a hormonal travesty that inspired a childlike tantrum or two, things were looking pretty good. So what right had I to fall apart?

For most anxiety-free onlookers, an emotional breakdown is understandable and totally justified for someone who has gone through something truly awful, but my inner turmoil only got worse when people said things like: "What have you got to feel down about?" or "But you look fine." I couldn't answer these questions, and I felt awful for my inability to just snap out of it given how good things *should* have been.

And then there were the statements, which I'm sure were meant to be helpful (they were *not*), such as: "But look at how worse off you could be," "You've so much going for you," "If only you could see how good you have it."

And that's precisely where we need to cut the crap: Our contemporary experience of anxiety is not dependent on something terrible that threatens our survival, nor is it a members-only club for people who've been dragged through the emotional trenches. Though arguably more common among teens and those in their twenties, anxiety is also not age-specific. Sure, awful life events will certainly throw a bad bout of stress and anxiety right in your face, but even the most fortunate among us can find ourselves floored by a tsunami of fear and worry. Yes, there will always be someone worse off, and if that kind of perspective improves your feelings of anxiety then great. But remember this: It's all relative. *You* feel like crap, right now. What you certainly don't need is the added feeling that you have no right to feel like crap. That's bullsh*t.

The thing is, however, that even though we've evolved significantly in certain ways, our brains—and our bodies—react to stress in the same way they did when we were chasing down hyenas in the wild for our Sunday roast, and that's arguably where evolution (our nervous systems have been evolving for 600 million years) needs to hurry the f*ck up. Your brain just can't tell the difference between running away from a predator and a boss or a bully whose footsteps make you shudder in fear, nor can it tell if you're rich or on the breadline. It doesn't need specifics about what the threat *is*, it just produces the necessary hormones for your survival, regardless of what's going on.

It's still the same brain that reacts in all cases.

To make this as clear a picture as possible, I've recruited the help of clinical psychologist Dr. Coyne, who has the lowdown on your basic brain chemistry. So prepare yourself for a brief dip into the scientific terminology pool but worry not—it makes sense. She explains:

> The most important players when it comes to anxiety are the prefrontal cortex, the amygdala, the hippocampus, the stress hormones and the stress regulatory systems. The prefrontal cortex is the part of the brain that enables us to think, reason, plan ahead, weigh up our options, show concern for others and calm ourselves when we perceive danger. The prefrontal cortex is the higher thinking part of the brain that has grown dramatically in the course of human evolution and differentiates us from other mammals. The lower part of the brain, called the sub-cortex, is our primitive animal brain which has evolved relatively little.
>
> Originally defined by French physician Paul Broca as a series of subcortical structures surrounding the border between the cerebral hemispheres and the brainstem, the limbic system includes the memory and motivation components of emotion. Located directly behind each ear, one of its star players is a walnut-shaped structure called the amygdala, which governs emotions and triggers alarm signals of fear in the brain. The amygdala directly interacts with its neighboring structure, and another star player, called the hippocampus. Together, they connect an emotion to an event leading to a release

of stress hormones that increases the brain and body's arousal. (Not the good kind of arousal, unfortunately.)

As it swings into action, the limbic system influences our endocrine system (these are hormone-secreting ductless glands) and the autonomic nervous system (ANS), composed of the sympathetic nervous system and the parasympathetic nervous system. The autonomic nervous system is a division of the peripheral nervous system that influences the function of internal organs.

The sympathetic nervous system is often considered the fight-or-flight system, while the parasympathetic nervous system is often considered the rest-and-digest system; hence they have "opposite" actions, where one system activates a physiological response and the other inhibits it.

In other words, the parasympathetic nervous system is your ally—it's the sympathetic counterpart that needs some work.

Problems arise because the amygdala performs a bit like an overly sensitive burglar alarm; it can get a little overactive and think you're in danger when you're really just fine (blame the ancient circuitry from when our ancestors were faced with several life-or-death decisions a day). It can also trigger long after you've endured something stressful (more on that in Chapter 2).

Per Dr. Coyne:

> Furthermore, the amygdala is one of the brain's many memory systems—also known as a "sloppy" emotional memory system—in that it fires a lot even when there is no actual threat. So, if something in the present is remotely similar to something you found frightening in the past, it can trigger negative feelings and memories of frightening images, sensations and impressions from the past.

So, words that sound like dinosaur names aside, that all made sense, right? If not, this diagram should help:

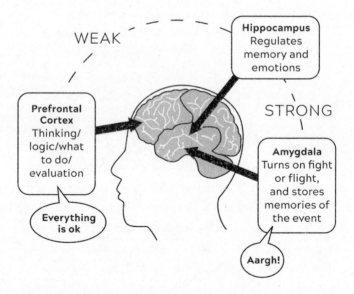

Where this goes beyond one easily isolated and fearful event, however, is the fact that these stress signals can be so strong, over a long period of time, that, as Dr. Coyne says, "they hijack the prefrontal cortex in such a way that all thoughts become tinged with fear and alarm."

This is where things went wrong for me.

What starts as a little nudge from your body to say, "Hey, I don't like this" (which for me was usually a stomachache), eventually becomes an avalanche of your overactive amygdala. If you've been worrying a lot over a long period of time and dealing with significant feelings of stress (significant to YOU), your prefrontal cortex is essentially exhausted (hence my inability to reassure myself that I wasn't allergic to water), while your amygdala is trigger happy, firing off warnings left, right and center. Under normal circumstances, the hippocampus regulates the production of cortisol because of its many stress hormone receptors. However, an overproduction of cortisol can impair the ability of the hippocampus both to encode and recall memories accurately. Not ideal.

On the other hand, the good news is that if this higher part of your brain is functioning well—and that's our task here—Dr. Coyne says "it can moderate a strong fear, calming both the body and the lower brain by releasing soothing chemicals, which will calm your thoughts."

What's more, you can train your higher brain (in other words, you can empower your reasoning prefrontal cortex) to recognize the warning signs well before any strong feelings of fear or panic arise, which will calm the amygdala. This is a concrete and crucial step in tilting the balance toward the reasoning part of your brain.

In my own experience, this information alone was a huge relief: it wasn't my fault that I felt this way. It wasn't my fault that I couldn't just snap out of it.

I couldn't help the fact that all of my thoughts were tinged with fear; it was simply a result of my worn-out prefrontal cortex that simply needed a little patience from me and some TLC. It's the same for you.

With this understanding of the brain, when I was subsequently caught up in a bad patch, I was able to then step back and say, "Okay, you're feeling quite anxious for no apparent reason, and things that wouldn't normally make you fearful suddenly seem overwhelming, but this is why." Give yourself some time, accept that this is how your body functions, and know that all will be well.

By being mindful of the inner workings of your brain, as well as the outer mechanisms, that promote anxiety and fear, you can already reduce their effects.

Chapter summary

- *Anxiety is not all in your head, nor is it a "mood" that you're in.*

- *Anxiety is a physiological result of your body trying to protect you.*

- *Stress and anxiety are necessary for your survival.*

- *Though we no longer face the same threats as our prehistoric ancestors, our brains still function much the same way, which is annoying.*

- *Wrapping your head around basic brain chemistry is an effective tool in itself.*

- *Though your suffering might pale in comparison to that of others, it's all relative to your own brain.*

Figuring out why you are here

IF YOU'RE FEELING "suddenly" very anxious or you've had your first earth-shattering panic attack, then to your frantic and fragile mind, it might feel as though it's come entirely out of the blue. Chances are, it hasn't. To understand why you are feeling like the dog's dinner, you first need to learn how to adopt a "helicopter view" of your life, which, in psychology terms, simply refers to stepping back, taking yourself out of one specific moment, and objectively observing the bigger picture.

By its very nature, anxiety causes us to home in on and obsess irrationally about specifics and details, rather than observing a calmer, more holistic picture of our situation. (By the way, when I use the word "holistic," I mean looking at the whole body—physical, psychological and social factors, all of which are inter-connected and have a combined effect on our well-being. Try not to associate the term "holistic" with any preconceived ideas about "new-age mumbo jumbo.")

As I explained in Chapter 1, my early experiences of acute stress were channeled entirely through my digestive system, leaving me in the most intense discomfort on a daily basis. Because, at first, it didn't feel like "typical" anxiety—I wasn't feeling fearful or particularly nervous—naturally, all I (and the GPs I visited) could focus on was my stomach, trying to treat this one isolated part of my body. However, as my sore stomach was merely a symptom of a wider problem—anxiety—nothing I did that was specifically for my tummy made a blind bit of difference. It wasn't my gut that needed treating, nor was there anything actually wrong with it. It was the mounting stress, which eventually turned into hideous anxiety, that needed to be resolved.

I'll delve into a bit more detail on the incredibly eye-opening links between our gut and our minds in Chapter 17, but for now, I want you to consider your own habits of thinking with your blinkers on—and, don't worry, we only really begin to take a "helicopter view" approach when we're faced with something like this, so at least you'll know how to from now on.

For most people who are suffering with acute anxiety, there are several factors at play, and that's precisely why you need to take that psychological back-step so that you can get an aerial view of both your physical health and your lifestyle. With time, patience and an open mind, what might at first have seemed like a bolt of sh*tty lightning will start to make sense.

So, more about my own experience.

Eventually, when I took a moment to stop obsessing over yet another food group to which I wrongly assumed I had become horribly allergic, I had a sort of lightbulb moment (with the help of Caolan, a friend who's like a therapist who doesn't charge). I realized that while nothing horrendous had happened in my life, I had made a few big changes in relatively quick succession that had, perhaps, left me a little more vulnerable than I was aware of, and so it hadn't taken much more than a prolonged period of stress to push me over the edge from the kind of stress I could brush off to the kind of anxiety where I just shut down. Completely.

At first, it really was just stress, and had I been able to identify it as that, I may not have fallen quite so hard. But the way I look at it now, it probably would have wound up happening later on.

(Side note: This might sound bizarre, but I'm honestly relieved—*so* relieved—that I went through this in my mid-twenties, so that I'm now equipped to deal with any stresses that will emerge later in life—you'll get to this point, too.)

Bearing in mind that every person's experience of anxiety is different, as are everyone's reasons for suffering, I'm going to explain briefly where I was at when my anxiety began. It's far from a dramatic story.

After a hectic Christmas, most of which I spent trying to keep up with my social life while battling with a really woeful flu, I moved out of my family home. Though I was really excited to move in with my boyfriend, I had always been the most homebird-iest of homebirds and though everyone else at the same age seemed to want to spread their wings and go as far away as possible, I just didn't. I was so emotionally dependent on my mother that if I ever felt unwell, I needed her to be there in order to feel better. That need to be soothed by your mother is something most people get over as they approach their twenties, but admittedly, today, I feel no different. She was and is my emotional comfort blanket.

So, I moved in with my boyfriend and, though I was loving my independence, perhaps I was going through some sort of subconscious adjustment period, separating my emotional idea of home from the physical home I had grown up in. Then, within the space of just a few weeks, I changed jobs, too. At the time, I was working as an editor for a successful online publication, the same place where, a few years earlier, I had started as an intern, fresh out of college. It was the job I'd always dreamed of—the people made it even better—and I couldn't believe my luck. I had learned so much and my confidence was sky-rocketing.

Then came an offer I couldn't refuse. It was a start-up company on the cusp of greatness, and they wanted me at the editorial helm. I was incredibly flattered but, deep down, I was doubtful about whether or not I was cut out for start-up life (I'd grown used to working as efficiently as possible and was still managing to clock off at a reasonable hour). Doubts aside, at that point, I had already made it to the role of editor in my current job, and so, with my ambition bursting at the seams, there was nowhere left for me to go. Though I loved what I did, I thought I needed to keep challenging myself. I thought it was a bad idea to get comfortable.

In retrospect, this was a little too harsh. You don't have to spend your life constantly pushing yourself from the frying pan into the fire; if you're enjoying something, just keep doing it.

I was nervous to leave such a good role, but I decided to just "feel the fear and do it anyway." What's the worst that could happen? There was so much excitement surrounding my job change. The media scene in Ireland is relatively small, and this new company suddenly had everyone's attention, so my joining them was industry news.

Though there was nothing awful about the job or the company, the dynamic just didn't suit me, sensitive creature that I am. And I guess, with my batteries already running a little lower than usual, and the added upheaval of moving house, I was more fragile than I knew. I was functioning at a 6 or 7, so it wasn't going to take very much to push me over the edge. Measuring your anxiety and stress levels on a scale from 1 (totally relaxed) up to 10 (full-blown panic attack), you should aim for a normal base level of 3–4. It's not possible to be at a 1 all day every day, so don't even try it.

When your base level climbs to 6–7, you are becoming more and more sensitive to stressors (internal thoughts and fears and external stimuli). At this point, you might not feel too bad but all it takes is a little more stress to blow your anxiety level right up to a 9 or 10, setting you up for a panic attack, which feels as though it's come out of nowhere. It hasn't.

But this job *had* to work out. I had blabbered on about how excited I was all over social media. I had left my cushy role, and I'd already been replaced. I couldn't take it back. I couldn't just decide "this isn't for me." Quitting was not an option. Giving up was, I thought, just an incredibly irrational and dramatic suggestion that I tried really hard to bury.

And actually, my subconscious did a really good job of the burying: "Don't even *think* about *thinking* about that," it might as well have said. I could not turn around to my family and my boyfriend and say, "Well, actually, I made a mistake." What would I do? How would I pay my rent? Or bills?

I told myself things like, "It'll get better, I'll start to really like it. These things always take three months or so to settle. I just have to get used to it. It's normal to feel a bit panicked at first." What I should have done was have a proper, real conversation with myself or someone close to me, but I felt so silly for even thinking this way.

One morning, about a month into the role, I woke up feeling uneasy. I had to get a grip. Looking around, my friends were handling all kinds of intense jobs, and they were thriving—it's just what we have to do, right? And the other team members who'd joined this company at the same time as me seemed to be killing it, too. "Why can't I just suck it up? Very few people actually love their job, that's a luxury, and I'm a grown-up and I have to earn money, and you've gone and made this decision now so just SHUT UP."

Instead of airing my concerns, I tried to just go with the flow and, as is a common trait of the Irish, say nothing. It didn't work. My stomach was saying, "Nope, I don't like this." (Yes, I do like to give voices and personalities to various parts of my body, it helps me make sense of its behaviors.) But my conscious mind was having none of it. I was all messed up.

Then came the fruitless obsession with fixing my stomach problems, because I certainly wasn't about to admit that maybe, just maybe, I'd misjudged my career move. While out loud I said, "I just have no idea why I'm so sick all of a sudden"—and I really did think that—a very tiny, very quiet part of me couldn't help but draw a correlation between starting a new job and suddenly feeling ill. Admitting this, however, was, as far as I was concerned back then, admitting weakness. If I was really sick because I couldn't handle my new job, what did that say about me? Was I really that weak? I felt ashamed by this perceived weakness.

It got worse and worse and worse until my body realized that I wasn't quite getting the message with the stomach issues, so it threw something else in the mix that I'd never before experienced: severe panic attacks. I vividly remember the first one (they're generally hard to forget).

I was in bed, crying about how inexplicably awful I felt, and I started googling my symptoms. As far as I could see, everything pointed toward ovarian cancer. I just lost it. I started to shake and I couldn't calm myself. Eventually, I fell asleep, worn out, and woke up the next day still reeling from the trauma of it. I tried to pull myself together and go to work, but then I broke down again on the way there, crying and feeling panicked. I rang my mum, telling her that I wasn't okay and that I didn't know what was going on.

Though I know my way around Dublin city like the back of my hand—I've never lived anywhere else—I was suddenly very disoriented and couldn't figure out where I was. I just couldn't put one foot in front of the other anymore. The next day, again, I tried to reassure myself that maybe I'd just had a really weird few days, and so I went out for dinner with my boyfriend. He had become wary of how sensitive I seemed to be and asked if I was sure I felt up for it. To me, though, if I said I *wasn't* up for it, that meant admitting that I was not okay—mentally—and that just sounded absurd. Perhaps it was ignorance on my part, but I was nowhere near that essential point of realization, when the inextricable link between our minds and our bodies can no longer be ignored. I'd never known of anyone to suffer so physically from a psychological concept such as stress. I told him I was fine, because I wanted to be fine, and I thought that if I said it, I would be.

And so we went out for dinner, but at this point—and this is the only way I've ever really been able to articulate the feeling—it felt as though I had just lost the invisible protective defence layer that I like to think we're all born with. A similar analogy might be to imagine if the Earth suddenly had no ozone layer whatsoever, rendering every inch of our planet incredibly vulnerable. I was suddenly so much more sensitive to all external stimuli, from loud noises on the TV to people saying hello in person. On the way to the restaurant, we bumped into a friend who merely stopped to say hello, as normal people do. I wasn't expecting to bump into anyone in my fragile state. I said hello and smiled on the outside, while on the inside my brain was screaming at me: "If I have to stand here for one more minute and make small talk I'm actually going to die." I was allergic to everything that surrounded me, overwhelmed by it all.

This realization was, in a word, sh*t. After we'd gone into the restaurant and my boyfriend was, again, looking at me like he didn't recognize me—he was just worried, of course—I broke down, pouring more tears than I thought I was capable of producing right into my bowl of ramen noodles, much to the concern of our waiter. At the time, I couldn't wrap my head around what was happening to me, the only thing I felt was fear and nothing made sense. If I could have bought a return ticket back into my mum's womb, I would have.

Shortly thereafter, when I was inevitably forced to confront the "helicopter view" of my life, I could see that I had been simply holding on to and resisting the stress in my body for far too long, which is why all hell broke loose on the inside.

From a hormonal perspective, my body was in overdrive when it came to cortisol production (the stress hormone), so even though I now said, "Okay, I can't really deny what's going on here anymore," at that stage I'd already put my body through too much, and so it wasn't going to be a simple case of "snapping out of it" with this realization alone.

That weekend, I made a decision to give myself a break for *maybe* just a week. This was the first stage of accepting that all was not okay. Unfortunately, a week off wasn't going to do it.

As you are reading this, your anxiety might be early enough that you can deal with it swiftly, before it gets out of hand, but, as I said, I was in quite a bad way physically and emotionally at this point, and soon realized after that breakdown in the restaurant that I wasn't well enough to work at all. I needed to remove any potential stressors, such as the stress of trying to be okay in an office when I just wasn't, and let myself be. I needed time, lots of time, to come back to zero and focus on the basics.

Throwing in the towel was a really difficult choice to make, but luckily I had the support of my friends and family (we'll be exploring the importance of relationships more in Chapter 13), and I was finally able to accept it. My well-being had to come first, and to this day, it still does. I was going to be okay, according to everyone else; if only I believed it myself at the time.

So, in a very long-winded way, that's how I personally wound up in the grips of crippling anxiety. Nothing major, just too much change too quickly, and, more specifically, change that I didn't like. That was the simple straw that broke the camel's back.

I hope, at this point, you're starting to nod to yourself, identifying what it might have been for you. And just to reiterate, it really doesn't have to be anything dramatically or negatively life-altering—you have every right to feel overwhelmed and anxious, whatever the reasons, whatever your age. Whatever you're experiencing is relative to you. If anyone tells you otherwise, they're a dick. Agreed?

Childhood experiences

What was also potentially at play were past experiences—again, there was nothing bad—but I had definitely been an anxious kid, and certainly an anxious teen. While these days I don't like to focus too much of my energy on trundling back through my childhood—in the sense that I'm not sure what I can really do about it now—it certainly does help to look back briefly with open eyes. After all, logic and reasoning aren't things we fully develop until we're past the age of eleven, so if we experienced anything unnerving before reaching that age, we wouldn't have been likely to rationalize or make absolute sense of it.

At the same time, however, what we form before our concept of logic is our memory, which develops rapidly between the ages of two to seven, and it's in that time where a lot of what we perceive can affect us later in life. For many people, anxiety that manifests itself when they are an adult has been lying dormant since childhood. For me, I was always complaining of feeling sick, and now that I've grown up, I can clearly see the link between my feeling sick and my being afraid, as kids often are.

Speaking of her passionate interest in the emerging field of infant mental health, Dr. Coyne talks about how rapid advances in neuroscience are showing us that, in addition to genetics, brain development is an experience-dependent social process; hence early social and emotional experiences between birth and three years of age actually *shape* a child's brain. Given that 80 percent of a child's brain is formed by the age of three, and given the significant impact of early-life experience on the formation of crucial brain pathways, this has serious implications for the origins of anxiety.

Dr. Coyne explains that early-life experiences of stress over-activate the brain's fight-or-flight response, which is an evolutionary adaptation that pulls us toward aggression (fight) or avoidance (flight), and away from the calm soothing of the higher brain:

> The more fear a person has experienced in their lives at a young age, the more trigger-happy their amygdala is.
>
> If an aspect of the person's present situation reminds them of an emotionally painful image or event from their past (particularly childhood), the amygdala can register it as an actual repeat of that painful situation, without the person knowing that they are only remembering something. The person will think their fear is justified by something in the present which is in fact totally benign.

Now, I suspect that if you're reading this, you're older than age eleven (if not, bravo) but it's worth noting when it comes to having kids of your own. Perhaps, if those around me had recognized my stomach pains for what they really were and intervened at an age when things were still in the process of being molded, my experiences later in life may have been different. This is something we've only really begun to be aware of in recent years and hopefully, for today's kids, we will more readily identify when they're simply feeling anxious (they themselves won't be able to label it as that, of course), and so reduce their experience of anxiety as an adult. For people of my generation and beyond, there just wasn't enough information out there; it's nobody's fault. But all is not lost.

Delayed reactions to bad experiences

It is also worth being mindful of the fact that, for many, acute anxiety that presents itself at a time when everything seems to be going just fine is often our bodies' delayed reaction to something we experienced not so long ago.

I liken this to how we might deal with having the flu, for example. Have you ever noticed how, even when you're incredibly busy and stressed you're able to hold things together and get the job done, and then, the minute you relax or go on holiday (typical), slowly beginning to unwind, your defense system lets its guard down (after all, you can't expect to hold strong twenty-four-seven) and suddenly you get sick? This, I believe, is a huge factor in relation to anxiety, too.

So maybe you have gone through something really horrible, such as losing a family member. And, testament to your resilience, you held yourself together during one of life's most trying times, because your body was there for you, giving you every bit of strength it could muster to get you through. Then, when you got beyond the point of merely going through the motions, or going from A to B, and when you stopped worrying about everyone else, your body and mind finally had a chance to say, 'Hey, I need a break too.'

It might be hard to identify the link at first, because you'll no doubt tell yourself you were okay through everything that happened; chances are, this is more than likely why.

Unless you are a complete rarity in that your mind really does operate independently of your body—I'd like to know what your secret is—your body will always speak your mind, even if there's a bit of time delay. If you don't want to take my word for it, read Debbie Shapiro's *Your Body Speaks Your Mind*; she said it first.

Contemporary lifestyles

Beyond our own individual circumstances for suffering, I feel quite strongly that one of the most prevalent reasons for our collective experience of anxiety is our contemporary lifestyles. Seriously, so many more people are suffering than you might realize. They're either keeping silent or they haven't yet been able to identify it (you can lend them this book when you're done).

We're encouraged to be our best selves, to pass with flying colors, to outdo ourselves at work, "to feel the fear and do it anyway," take the risk, maintain colorful social lives, kill it at the gym, hold down many fulfilling relationships, increase our following on social media by being really witty several times a day, look after our health, look after our figures, look after our mental health, among many other to-dos—Christ, that's a lot of pressure at any given time on one person. I'm even exhausted just listing it and, for many, that's a list that's got to be checked off daily. We were never designed to have this many plates spinning and though I'm glad we're no longer responsible for hunting our own food, if you're that tough on yourself for long enough, one of those plates is bound to drop. Isn't our quest for perfection and having it all oddly correlated to the rising epidemic of stress and anxiety? It's certainly food for thought, that's for sure.

And that brings this chapter to a close. I'm no psychic, so, without knowing you, I can't quite tell you the precise reason, or combination of reasons, why you're here, feeling like an omelette dropped on the floor, but I can empathize.

The figuring out part you'll have to do on your own but the exercises below should help. Hopefully by now, however, you're sitting comfortably in the pilot seat of your own helicopter—don't be afraid to look down—and the pieces of the puzzle are starting to come together.

Maybe it's a childhood experience rearing its ugly head, maybe it's a lot of change at once, maybe it's mounting stress that you've been enduring for too long, maybe it's a bad breakup from your first love that you thought you were fine about but maybe, months later, you're not. Maybe it's a simple case of too much caffeine (which we'll explore in Chapter 17) or maybe it's a combination of everything. The point here, I firmly believe, is that there is a reason for it, so please don't, not for one second, feel like you're losing your mind. All is well.

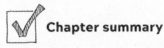 **Chapter summary**

- *Stand back. Adopt the "helicopter view" of your own life and be as honest as you possibly can be with yourself about what might be contributing to your anxiety. Even if it feels like a silly reason or too small, make a note of it.*

- *You do not need to endure something traumatic to justify experiencing prolonged anxiety.*

- *Delayed reactions to difficult times are often a trigger for anxiety, even if it feels out of the blue.*

- *Your childhood can play a significant role in your experience of anxiety later on but it's not too helpful to dwell on the past now.*

- *Our contemporary lifestyles are often enough of a trigger for anxiety alone, without anything really bad having happened.*

- *Even a small amount of stress, when persistent and ignored, can add up in your body, resulting in more acute periods of ongoing anxiety.*

- *There is a reason for your feelings of anxiety, you just have to figure out what it is.*

Exercise
PSYCHOLOGICAL FORMULATION

To figure out why you're here, grab a pen and your personal workbook and get to work with your own "psychological formulation" exercise, which I've put together with Dr. Coyne.

This exercise is similar to something a clinician trained specifically in the area of mental health would do, but being able to formulate your own case can be hugely beneficial in ascertaining your own difficulties.

Psychological formulation involves turning your personal narrative into a manageable and meaningful synopsis to add perspective to your situation. For clinicians, this is a crucial part of the assessment process as it gathers all the information they need to help inform a suitable treatment plan.

There are two common models that can help organize the conceptual backbone of a formulation: the Bio-Psycho-Social Framework and the Four Ps model.

The Bio-Psycho-Social Framework is a tool that psychologists use to examine how psychological disorders develop and are maintained. The "bio" component of this theory examines aspects of biology that influence health, such as genetics, brain changes, illness or injury. The "psycho" component looks at psychological components, including the crucial interaction between thoughts, feelings and behaviors. The "social" component examines social factors, including interactions with others, culture and socio-economic status. The reason this model is so popular is that each element is connected and affects the other (e.g., your biological state can affect your psychological well-being and social interactions, and vice versa). Hence, psychological formulation rests on this idea of biological, psychological and social aspects all having a significant and interactive impact on your life.

The Four Ps model—Predisposing, Precipitating, Perpetuating, and Protective factors—is a simpler way of constructing a psychological formulation.

Have a look at the diagram below. Then, recreate this template in your journal and fill in the boxes with your own personal factors.

Predisposing factors **"Why me?"** *For example: Genetic vulnerability, early-life experiences, personality trait; core beliefs, such as "I'm not worthy"*	Precipitating factors **"Why now?"** *For example: Triggering events, illnesses or injuries, life-cycle adjustments, or transitions*

Presenting difficulties
List your current problems / diagnosis

Perpetuating factors **"Why does it continue?"** *For example: Thoughts, feelings, behaviors that maintain the problem, such as severity, avoidance*	Protective factors **"What can I rely on?"** *For example: Personal strengths, coping strategies, social support, capacity to seek support*

When filling out this diagram, be mindful of all aspects of your life, among which any of the following may be a contributing factor:

- Career
- Relationships
- Physical health
- Recent changes
- Childhood experiences
- Painful memories throughout life
- Drastic change in diet/alcohol consumption

The less sh*t side of anxiety

GOOD ANXIETY? Is there such a thing? Well, yes, there really is. And allowing for this more positive, open-minded perspective on anxiety—though I know it's hard at first— is another step on the road to owning it, managing it, showing it who's boss and using it to your advantage.

When you're suffering with acute anxiety, and your body just needs a holiday from, well, itself (I remember someone suggesting a break away to the countryside, and I thought, unless I could literally set up camp in someone else's super-chilled-out body, I had nowhere to go; the anxiety would always come along, uninvited), it's hard to imagine a time when you'll ever embrace how you feel. You want rid of it. If someone said they could turn off your body's stress response, you'd take it without question (but that, of course, would have dire consequences; our survival and even our energy each day depends on it). So, something I want you to start thinking about is knowing that while your anxiety might feel like a curse right now, in the not-too-distant future, you'll be such a master of your own anxiety that you'll be able to make it work *for* you rather than *against* you. You might even see it as a blessing in disguise.

Here's what anxiety gave me (well, the good parts).

High standards

My tendency toward anxiety is quite often propelled by a need to do well, to produce the goods and be at the top of my game, and so on. If I wasn't such a high achiever—or, rather, afraid of failure—I might not be the anxious person that I am. Now I'm not an Olympic gold medalist or a Nobel Prize-winner but without my anxious nature, I might not have done as well in school or in university, arriving at the point today where I'm doing what I love. Because of this fear, I believe I can do a better job than I ever would, had I no worries at all.

Work ethic

People with whom I work (I am now a freelance journalist) are often surprised by how fast I get things done or how many plates I might have spinning at one time, and they comment on my work ethic. Believe me, though, this work ethic is fueled by my anxiety. But it's the good kind of anxiety. And even now that I have a handle on it, if I was facing a big project—such as writing this book— and felt no jitters at all, I'd actually be concerned. It's my motivation.

A pattern to rely on

Instead of ever trying to reach a point where I'd be as cool as James Franco, before a big presentation, for example, I learned to recognize my pattern, and how it actually works for me. Feeling anxiety doesn't mean I'm not able, it means I've entered that mode of preparation.

Today, if it's something as unnerving as public speaking, here's how it might go: I agree to something, I get that initial "F*CK" feeling, I go through all of the doubts and reasons not to do it, and hope a manhole will open up right under my feet. Then, as the event approaches, I produce the necessary adrenaline, and my fear helps to ensure that I'm super prepared—then I do it, and it's fine. I then breathe a sigh of relief as the adrenaline starts to dissipate. Assuming I didn't accidentally expose a nipple while speaking, or something equally as horrendous that could happen to you on stage, I might even be on a bit of a high.

The key here, though, is not to say, "Okay, well, I've done that now so I'll never feel nervous doing that again." What if I do feel a bit jittery the next time? A few years ago, I might have freaked out tenfold, thinking there was something wrong with me and that I should just go and live in an igloo. "Here's the anxiety again, just give up." The thing is, I sure as hell *would* feel it, but that wouldn't mean I wasn't capable.

I might not feel quite as nervous, the more experience I get at doing something, but I will always have that little rumbling (sometimes it can be a loud f*cking roar) and I'll say, "Ah, there you are, here to make sure I do a good job." Oddly, its presence gives me confidence.

As we'll explore in more detail in Chapter 10, when we get to a point where we stop thinking about our anxiety as the enemy, and more as something that triggers the motivation to prepare us for an event (I like to think of it as that confidence-giving potion from Harry Potter, Felix Felicis), we reduce its physiological impact.

Self-awareness

Because of my sensitive nature and my anxiety experiences, I am now, by default, incredibly in tune with my body. This is hugely beneficial for obvious reasons. And it's because I understand what's going on that I'm no longer caught off-guard by things. I just instinctively know when something's off, when I should take a step back or when something isn't right for me. I really listen to my body now and take regular opportunities to activate that helicopter view we mentioned earlier. Obviously, life will still throw many things at me that I can't see coming—I am not in possession of a crystal ball—but as and when it does, I am able to recognize the signs and symptoms and expressions of this new experience in my mind and body.

Having an awareness of our vulnerability is crucial. While you don't want to walk around every day thinking about the worst that could happen, you also don't want to be so ignorant as to think that you are invincible, worsening your anxiety when life—inevitably—does bite you in the ass.

We are all sensitive, vulnerable creatures, and when we are aware of this and look after ourselves (though, obviously, not in an obsessive hypochondriac way), we manage everything better. It's about having your eyes open. Really open.

Anxiety awareness in others

Another thing that my anxiety experience has given me is an ability to talk to friends and family about things they may not yet be able to identify in themselves.

It's unfortunate but true; unless someone has experienced anxiety, it freaks them out, which reinforces the stigma that anxiety is something to be embarrassed about or ashamed of.

As my friend Caolan (just call him my guru) did for me when I was the one who was disillusioned, I am now able to reassure my nearest and dearest (and hopefully you too) that there's a very plausible reason for the overwhelming feeling of anxiety they're experiencing. The number of times I smile and nod (in recognition, not pleasure, obviously) as someone tells me their story and wonders why they've wound up feeling as though they're struggling to keep their head above water. Comforting them and helping them to realize that everything makes sense—again, your family needn't have been hit by a meteorite to justify your feelings—is in turn comforting for me.

Overcoming the stigma surrounding mental health

When you get to the point where you're feeling good again, living your life to the fullest and owning your anxiety, the real gift of this kind of experience is the opportunity to make a difference to the wider world by speaking up about how okay it is to not feel okay. When we reach the point where everyone is comfortable voicing their struggles, whatever they may be, the added weight of anxiety surrounding these struggles will be halved. Why? Because a huge portion of our anxiety is in itself fueled by what others will think of us and by what it might say about us.

Chapter summary

- *Looking at anxiety from a more positive perspective—even though this will be difficult at first—will help to change your relationship with anxiety so that it stops affecting you in such a negative way.*

- *If you experience anxiety, you're incredibly in tune with your body and self-aware. This is a good thing.*

- *Anxiety can help you to do better in certain situations. It can fuel your work ethic.*

- *Anxiety isn't always a bad thing.*

- *Anxiety can help you to have more empathy for others.*

- *Through experiencing anxiety, we can collectively overcome any stigma that still surrounds it.*

 **Exercise**
WHAT HAS ANXIETY GIVEN YOU?

Write down as many personal experiences as you can where your anxiety might have helped you, such as nailing a presentation. This will help you to start changing your relationship with your anxiety, removing its initially petrifying horns. Try to think of three things for each of the following questions.

1. What has anxiety gifted to you?
2. What key messages has it given you?
3. How has each experience impacted your view of anxiety?

CHAPTER
4

Understanding the negativity bias

ANOTHER INCREDIBLY HELPFUL assessment tool for me was an understanding of what's called the "negativity bias." Again, this is something you'll instantly recognize in your day-to-day behavior as it's something we all do— but, in the midst of a cycle of anxious thoughts, it can be hard to step back and say, "Ah, I see what's going on here." By the end of this chapter, you'll realize how essential this information is in relation to the treatment and management of your anxiety and, very quickly, you really will be saying, "I *do* see what's going on here," thus reducing the anxiety's effects.

In essence, the "negativity bias" refers to the way in which negative experiences weigh more heavily on the brain than positive ones. It's a hypothesis that's been proven time and time again in various studies, just give it a google. Why do we have it? Well, you can blame good old evolution for that one too; we've evolved to be fearful and acutely aware of the negative in order to sustain our survival.

Here's how it would have played out in a simpler (though considerably more terrifying) time. You're roaming the land to ensure you have the basics covered—you have to eat food and have sex (less so for fun, more so that you have children and can pass on your genes). You also have to avoid being eaten or killed by someone or something that wants your dinner. As explained by neuropsychologist Dr. Rick Hanson PhD, a leading authority on the negativity bias, back then, we were consistently deciding between approaching an "award" (food, procreation) and avoiding a "hazard" (angry lion). If you missed out on some food today, not to worry, you could always get more tomorrow. If you failed to avoid the wrath of Simba's Uncle Scar, however, you were toast. Hence, we had to place a lot more emphasis on the latter, and so our brains developed in such a way as to produce far more neural activity (as in "get the hell out of here") with negative stimuli than with positive stimuli.

Today, as far as our brains are concerned, not much has changed. We are still heavily attuned to the strong possibility of a threat while, at the same time, underestimating our resources (thank you, modern-day life) to deal with them. What's more, we react to negative occurrences far more quickly than we do to positive things: say, for example, if you're a bit tired, drifting off into a daydream while driving. Your limbic brain needs to recognize the threat of a potential road accident in a split second, triggering your fight or flight response and jolting you into action before you're even fully aware of what's going on, whereas something equally positive would take considerably longer to register. This reaction in this situation, you'll no doubt agree, is very useful. Where evolution leaves us high and dry, however, is that once the alarm bell goes off, negative experiences and events get stored quickly in our memories. By contrast, positive experiences and events usually need to be held in awareness for much longer (roughly ten to fifteen seconds) to transfer from our short-term memory to long-term storage.

Such negative experiences have a much stronger influence on how we evaluate things, when compared to extremely positive information. A modern-day example would be that even though ninety-nine people liked your YouTube video and left encouraging comments, one person gave you the thumbs down and said that you suck. That one negative comment will be blown out of proportion, instantly sticking out in your mind and tainting your evaluation, despite the fact that ninety-nine others loved what you did. Another one: you're having your annual performance review with your boss. They talk you through your many inspiring strengths, but—and as is their job— they allude to one area for improvement. You leave their office feeling deflated, and the fact that they praised you in other areas doesn't do much to lift your spirits. It's okay, we've been wired to zero in on the one negative in a stream of information and de-emphasize the positive or, as Dr. Hanson puts it in his book, *Buddha's Brain: The Practical Neuroscience of Happiness, Love and Wisdom*: "Our brains are like Velcro for negative experiences and like Teflon for positive ones."

According to one particular study,[1] our collective negativity bias comes from both experience and innate predispositions, meaning there's a bit of nature *and* nurture at play. In fact, the negativity bias has even been shown to be active in babies as young as three months old. Furthermore, the negativity bias can be manifested in several different ways (bear with me through the lingo). The first is "negative potency" where negative entities are stronger than the equivalent positive entities. Pretty self-explanatory. The second is "steeper negative gradients," where the negativity of negative events grows more rapidly as we approach them in space or time, than the positivity of positive events. Think of your rising fear as you're about to jump out of a plane (not that I'd *ever* do that). The third is "negativity dominance" where combinations of negative and positive entities yield evaluations that are more negative than the algebraic sum of individual subjective valences would predict, which is a fancy pants way of describing the scenario above with your performance review.

How does this all relate to ongoing feelings of anxiety? Well, it's not just about external threats. Dr. Coyne explains how this negativity bias inevitably plays a significant role in our views about ourselves, in our emotions, in our ability to take in information and, crucially, in our decision-making:

> It is known that people who do not notice positive stimuli and who tend to talk about negative experiences more readily than positive ones are more likely to struggle with anxiety and depression. Left unchecked, the negativity bias can become a serious impediment to good mental health. The negativity bias and the tendency of the brain to overestimate threats are synonymous with anxiety, and hence are at the core of its treatment, such as Cognitive Behavioral Therapy (see Chapter 16). By learning to correctly identify this pattern, a person can answer it back, refute it over and over again, until it slowly diminishes over time and is replaced by more rational, balanced thinking.

For me, simply knowing that not all emotions are created equal was comforting; it took the pressure from me to stop berating myself for honing in on the not-so-fun aspects of my experience and my inability to place more emphasis on the positive. It became a useful recognition tool in that my higher brain could say, "Okay, all you can see right now is this black pit of despair, and that's because of the negativity bias. We are primed to go negative. Now, let's regain control of this wiring and try to give more weight to the positive."

This wasn't always easy but a gratitude diary—though it seemed like a stupid exercise at first—was a good way of balancing out the bias. Writing down a list of negatives, and then writing a corresponding positive for each negative, was a good way to alter my brain's perspective. Time to get the journal out.

It might seem trivial, but it's all about being consistently mindful of the ways in which we've long since functioned, and rewiring our brains so they don't give us any unnecessary sh*t. Explained further by Dr. Hanson:

> By bringing awareness to how your brain reacts to feeling threatened, you can stimulate, and therefore build up, the neural substrates of a mind that has more calm, wisdom and sense of inner strength. A mind that sees real threats more clearly, acts more effectively in dealing with them and is less rattled or distracted by exaggerated, manageable or false alarms.[2]

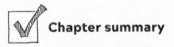 **Chapter summary**

- *You've been designed to focus on the negative, don't beat yourself up about it.*

- *Accept the fact that negative things weighing more heavily has been good for our survival.*

- *Accept the fact that negative things cause us to react more quickly and that they stay in our memory—more so than positive things.*

- *Make a conscious effort to draw your attention to the positive things you experience on a daily basis. Why? Because repeated patterns of brain activity change neural structure and function.*

Exercise 1
FINDING THE BALANCE

No matter how seemingly inconsequential, write down a list of positive experiences you've had today. This will help to bring your awareness to the things that aren't bad. Next, write down a list of negative thoughts—this is usually way easier for anxious folks—in one column. Next to that, write a list of positive thoughts to balance out the negative.

Positive Experiences	Negative Thoughts	Positive Thoughts
I enjoyed a long, hot shower.	I cooked a meal for my friends but one of them hardly touched her food.	Everyone else devoured their meal and one person even asked for the recipe!
I had a nice chat with the barista at the coffee shop, and my latte tasted even better.	**Negative brain says:** She hates it, she will think badly of me.	**Higher brain says:** It was nice food, you made an effort. You can't win 'em all.
I ate my lunch away from my desk with my phone on airplane mode.		

Exercise 2
COGNITIVE RESTRUCTURING[3]

Now that you are aware of the impact of your thoughts, you need to take a step back, suspend judgment and look at them logically.

Cognitive restructuring, or thought challenging, focuses on reducing your belief in unhelpful thoughts and finding alternative balanced thoughts that are more accurate and helpful. This is not about "thinking positively," it's about challenging thoughts fairly to create a more balanced view of the world.

Step 1: Identify the situation

Describe the situation that triggered your negative mood. Be as specific as possible.

Example: If you're someone who sees the world as a dangerous place, you might have fears of being hurt or robbed by a stranger. Stepping out of your house one day, you automatically think, "Today is the day I'll be attacked," which causes you to panic and run back inside.

Step 2: Analyze your mood

Write down the mood, or moods, that you felt during the situation. You can usually describe moods in one word, while thoughts are more complex.

Example: "Today is the day I'll be attacked" would be a thought, while the associated moods might be terror, anxiety, and powerlessness.

Step 3: Identify automatic thoughts

Make a list of the natural reactions, or "automatic thoughts," that you experienced in that situation.

Example: "There are a lot of dangerous people out there; I would make a good target . . ."

Step 4: Find objective supportive evidence

Write down any evidence you can find that supports the automatic thoughts you listed in Step 3. Your goal is to look objectively at what happened and write down specific events or comments that led to your automatic thoughts.

Examples: "I was on my own, which made it more likely for me to be attacked."

"I can predict when bad things are going to happen."

Step 5: Find objective contradictory evidence

Look rationally at your automatic thoughts and write down evidence that contradicts the thoughts. Consider other people's perspectives.

Examples: "I have walked on my own before and have not been attacked."

"There are no reports of such incidents in the area I live in."

Step 6: Identify fair and balanced thoughts

By this stage, in Steps 4 and 5, you've looked at both sides of the situation you described in Step 1. Take a balanced view about what happened and write down your new perspective. As you can see, these statements are fairer and more rational than the reactive thoughts.

Example: "I feel like something bad may happen, but

in reality the likelihood of something happening is extremely low and I am no more at risk than anyone else."

Step 7: Monitor your present mood

Take a moment to assess your mood and write down how you feel. Do you feel better about the situation? Next, reflect on what you could do about the situation. Is there any action you need to take or is it not as important as you initially thought?

Example: "I feel calmer. I will go out and feel proud of pushing through my fear."

Step 8: Create positive affirmations

Finally, create your own positive affirmations to counter negative thoughts and feelings in the future. Affirmations are positive, specific statements that enable you to visualize and believe in what you're affirming to yourself. They can help to raise your confidence and keep you motivated to achieve your goals. Align these with your core values.

Examples: "I am strong"; "I won't let my fears bring me down"; "I can push through my fear."

Owning your
vulnerability

IF, LIKE ME, you've devoured anything written by Elizabeth Gilbert, Brené Brown, Cheryl Strayed, or Arianna
Huffington (yep, feel-good nonfiction is my jam), you'll
recognize several of their pearls of wisdom woven
through my own learnings. Unbeknownst to them, these
guys were my teachers, my gurus, the comforting hug I
needed during my darkest hours (or, in the spirit of keeping it real, whenever my mum was out of reach). In fact, to
this day, Elizabeth Gilbert's *Eat Pray Love* remains fixed
to my bedside table in case I ever need a fast-acting dose
of "you've got this." (A word to the wise: just ignore the
film and go straight to the book; it was a game-changer
for me.)

There's a reason why these women are all TED-talking,
award-winning, bestselling authors—they're refreshingly

anti-bullsh*t and they talk a serious amount of sense, all of which is based on their own experiences, though each of them touches on the subject in their own way.

Brené Brown is arguably the most passionate advocate on the planet for embracing one's own vulnerability. She's an incredibly informed and accomplished social research professor, with over thirty years' experience on the subjects of vulnerability, courage, worthiness, and shame. Looking back over her various research projects (and she's by no means done yet), Brown has concluded wholeheartedly that if you're looking for one key roadblock in your quest for happiness, it's this: an unwillingness and/or fear to accept and embrace your innate vulnerability.

When you take a moment to look at those who are struggling or stuck, the theme of resisting one's vulnerability will emerge almost instantly. An example might be the more-than-capable guy whose music career won't take off until he's prepared to risk failure and vulnerability in the pursuit of success and contentment. Drilling down a little further on Brown's simple secret to happiness (well, on paper it sure *sounds* simple), I am more than confident that if we can conquer the fear of our own vulnerability and learn to embrace it, we can conquer— and yes, own—our anxiety, too.

Vulnerability goes hand in hand with anxiety; they're like peas in a pod. Specific personal circumstances aside, this whole nightmare came to the fore for me when my unrelenting stubbornness refused to back down in the face of my own vulnerability. I was terrified to admit that I was struggling, that I couldn't go at the pace that those around me seemed so fine with. I couldn't admit to my friends, family and peers that I was finding it hard to keep my head above water, because that would have been to admit weakness. I was supposed to have my sh*t together, I was supposed to be able for anything, to just suck it up and put it down to one—max two—bad days. I wasn't supposed to fall apart. The word "breakdown," as far as I was concerned, was reserved for "crazy" people. Most of all, I struggled to admit it to myself—and this fed the anxiety hugely.

Like our collective dependence on oxygen, vulnerability is something that we all have in common. There isn't one of us who is not vulnerable, either physically or emotionally, at some or many points in our lives. In fact, unless you live in a bulletproof, steel cocoon where nothing remotely fun or scary can ever happen, you're vulnerable on a daily basis. But despite the fact that vulnerability is one of those unavoidable tenets of the human experience, we also seem to share a fear of it. Particularly when it comes to emotional vulnerability.

Imagine sitting at a dinner party with the most ball-aching flu you've ever endured and having to put on a happy face, engage in conversation and laugh at unfunny jokes until such a time comes when you can escape. Not one person—unless of course they're an asshole devoid of all empathy, in which case you should find new friends to have dinner with—would think badly of you for saying, "Hey, I feel like crap, I'd really rather go to bed," but still, we struggle to admit this kind of vulnerability. We "power through it," we "don't give up," we suffer. Take that dinner party scenario and swap out the flu for a wave of anxiety—there's not a hope in hell you're about to say, "Guys, I'm feeling very overwhelmed right now, I just need a time out." Our society deems that admitting *that* level of vulnerability is, for some reason, far too socially risky, but what's the worst that could happen? Someone thinks less of you? The more we embrace and own our vulnerability, the sooner we break the stigma surrounding it and, therefore, cut out the needless inner turmoil.

Empathy is another quality that many of us share, but it's one we rarely give each other credit for: We struggle to reveal our vulnerability to other people for fear of what they'll think, while, at the same time, we overlook the likelihood that they will understand. We're human, we're empathetic by nature. Not only should another person be able to understand how you're feeling, chances are they'll have felt it too. In fact, if I had a dollar for every person who's emerged from the cracks to say, "Hey, me, too" when I've spoken openly about my own experience, I'd be loaded (okay, I might only have about 100 bucks).

Something doesn't make sense. Shouldn't our innate ability to empathize with one another negate our shared fear of vulnerability? Lest any of us have forgotten, we're all in this together.

In her book *Daring Greatly*, Brené Brown talks about how difficult it can be to own one's story, but that running away from it is even more difficult. When you embrace your vulnerability, and say (even if it's just to yourself to begin with), "Okay, I'm feeling anxious, I'm overwhelmed, I am physically suffering and I'm going to deal with it," then you can take active and emotional ownership of your situation.

The monster, now pacified, begins to retreat. It just does, because finally, you're allowing yourself to be you, you're giving yourself a break, you're giving your vulnerability a comforting glass of hot milk, reassuring this very important part of you that it deserves to be here just as much as confidence or any other preferential traits.

Another of my favorite pieces from this book talks about the importance of bravery—how the only way to discover the power of light is to explore the darkness.

Now, okay, on the surface, that might sound like some poetic BS, but it's anything but. Trust me. Letting your vulnerability, however, manifest itself at whichever point in your life you are at is *everything*. Get on board with this and the rest should come easy.

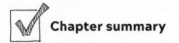 **Chapter summary**

- *We are all vulnerable. Period.*

- *Give up trying to be bulletproof; it's causing you more anxiety.*

- *Embracing our vulnerability is so important not just in terms of our personal happiness but in terms of managing our anxiety, too.*

- *Start by accepting your own vulnerability; show yourself some compassion. Then, trust that the people who matter will understand your feelings of vulnerability and will have felt them, too.*

- *Trust in people's ability to empathize with how you feel, the way you do for them.*

- *This is going to be one of your biggest roadblocks between a life defined by anxiety and one where it doesn't hold you back.*

 Exercise 1
OWNING YOUR VULNERABILITY

Even if you don't believe them right now, write down a list of realistic affirmations that help you to own your vulnerability. All that matters is that they relate to you and when you're feeling good, you could well believe them. Repeat them as often as you feel vulnerable. For example:

- · I am strong.
- · I accept myself as I am.

- I am comfortable with needing a helping hand.
- I am surrounded by people who accept my vulnerabilities.
- My anxiety tells me how much I care about what's important to me.
- My anxiety has given me more awareness of and empathy toward others.
- I am not afraid to expose my vulnerabilities.

Exercise 2
WHAT'S THE WORST THAT COULD HAPPEN?

Here is a psychological exercise, or "magic formula," that can help to reduce your feeling of anxiety and embrace your vulnerabilities. Here's how it breaks down in three steps:

1. Ask yourself: "What is the worst that could happen?"
2. Be willing and prepared to accept the worst if necessary.
3. Calmly try to figure out how to improve on the situation that you have accepted.

It takes practice to apply this technique, especially the second step, but it can help you to regain your calm. Imagining the worst-case scenario can actually make the reality feel a lot more manageable and also put your brain into problem-solving mode.

TOOL KIT

Quick Things You Can Jump To

How to deal with a panic attack in real time

OH HELLO, PANIC, nice of you to drop by.

When panic attacks

So, right now, you're in the midst of an anxiety attack. Good thing you bookmarked this page for such an occasion; this is one you can come back to as often as you need.

Breathing easy is a challenge, to say the least. As far as your body is concerned, the world is ending, you're in danger, and your caveman instincts want you to get out of there, stat. You don't know why this is happening.

You felt absolutely fine two minutes ago and, as far as you can see, there is no knife-wielding axe murderer in your vicinity. You're petrified that your mind has the power to yield this kind of influence over your body. Why can't you get it together? Why has your fight-or-flight response been triggered when you're sitting on your couch? More thoughts like this continue to flood your mind, serving only to worsen the feeling.

STOP.

Now is *not* the time for analysis. We can do that later when you're feeling better. This is the time to get you back to basics.

First: Breathe. Breathe in for a count of four (from your belly, not your chest), hold for a count of four, and release your breath over a count of four. Do it again. And again. If you can, resist the urge to exhale your breath forcefully by slightly tightening your throat so that the breath comes out slowly. You should hear a slight whooshing noise. This is the Ujjayi breathing technique, and it's very effective (more on that on page 157).

Second: Stop trying to resist the feeling of panic. Stop trying to (internally) run as far away from yourself as possible. Close your eyes (if you can) and let it happen to you. "Come at me, do your worst," is something I got used to saying. You are stronger than panic. Surrendering to your feelings of panic will instantly dissipate them; it's the resisting that makes it worse.

Inhale confidence. Hold for four. Exhale anxiety slowly. Hold for four.

Third (and by now it's probably already been and gone): Accept that it's happened. You've had a panic attack, yes, but nobody died. You can't go back in time and erase the experience, but you will get better and better at minimizing it, should it arise again. You're okay, there is no harm done and nothing bad is happening to you, nor will it happen to you as a result of a panic attack. Your body is trying its best to protect you, but it's gone a little overboard. (I know, that's putting it more than mildly.)

Again. Nice, long, slow breaths. Do this for as long as you like, and then come back to me.

You're back. Feel better?

I've been there. You can't quite appreciate the weight of a panic attack, or its ability to completely throw you off course for the rest of the day, until you've felt it yourself.

In my experience, panic attacks happened quietly on the inside—think of a duck gliding along the water looking as cool as a cucumber, meanwhile its legs are flapping frantically below the surface. Nobody around me would have suspected a thing. Instead of the need to breathe into a brown paper bag, the apex of my anxiety manifested itself as a burning fire that flooded my body. One time, I actually thought I had eaten something poisonous and was hours away from death. I wasn't—and now know how ridiculous that sounds in retrospect. My panic attacks didn't last very long—they never do—but they were horrendous enough to leave me reeling long after they'd finished.

On a physical level, what's happening is this: Your mind is under pressure, your thoughts are spiraling, through no fault of your own, and your body assumes it's under threat. It triggers your fight-or-flight response and, because there's nothing to flee from or fight, a combination of adrenaline and cortisol (the hormones you've been designed to release as a survival mechanism) just explodes inside you.

No fun, but, on a physical level, there's no harm done.

The aftermath

Finally, give yourself a break. This is the part that really got me. It wasn't so much the panic but the aftermath, when I'd cry and obsess over the fact that it had happened at all, coming to the conclusion that I'd just taken ten massive steps backwards. I hadn't, and neither have you.

Now that your breathing and heart rate have returned to normal, do not beat yourself up over the fact that you had a panic attack. You're not losing it, you're not weak, you're not choosing to do this to yourself. Be as nice to yourself as you would be to a friend who's having a hard time. You'd wrap your arms around them and just let them feel however it is they feel. Think of your body as an overprotective but well-meaning parent who just really wants to keep you safe. Don't berate it. Reassure it. You *are* okay, you appreciate its efforts to shield you from impending doom, but there's nothing to fear.

In the next step, you need to look at the various vulnerability factors that contributed to this momentary rise in anxiety. This always helped me to understand why I might have been having a particularly hard time.

- Are you overworked or overtired?
- Have you been feeling stressed out for a while?
- Are you under pressure to be feeling good right now?
- Are you under the weather?
- Are you upset about something?
- Are you hungover?
- Have you been eating a lot of sugar?
- Are there a lot of stimulants in the mix, e.g., coffee?

Now you need to deal with your body physically—for now, no alcohol, no caffeine, no sugar, no unnecessary stimulation of the nervous system, no more analysis. It's time to reset and soothe your parasympathetic nervous system.

It's in dealing with the aftermath that you'll learn and improve the most.

Instead of pressuring yourself to not have a panic attack—for some people this idea is enough to give them one—focus your efforts on the restoration of your equilibrium post-attack. Eventually, the fear will simply go out of the experience because you'll become really familiar with the unthreatening outcome, and, thus, the tendency to panic in the future will subside. In fact, I'd almost be glad it happened, if you can push yourself that far. In an ideal world, we'd never have to feel that way, but many of us do at some point in our lives. Think of it instead as just another experience that you've survived and one that you can learn from.

After my bouts of panic (which, at first, were acute and regular over the course of a few months, then becoming less and less frequent for about a year), when I felt as though I'd been dragged through a ditch, minus the mud, I treated myself like royalty and simply wrote off the day. Not in a negative way, but in a I'm-going-to-be-really-nice-to-myself-now kind of way. I'd go home, I'd tell my boyfriend about it, which had the effect of normalizing it, in the same way I'd tell him about anything else that happened in my day. "I had a really great sandwich for lunch. I went to Ikea. I had a panic attack . . ."—I wouldn't pretend it didn't happen, and I wouldn't be afraid to admit that I'd lost my nerve.

In the beginning, as most people who mean well do, he'd overreact and rush to my side. "Oh no, are you okay? That's awful," which would just freak me out even more. I soon realized that this probably wasn't helping; I didn't want or need an oh-my-God reaction. Instead, he learned to say, "Okay, babe, that's fine. Nothing to worry about, just a little blip. You're going to be fine, and you're already fine. Now, what would you like to do to make you feel better?"

The thing is, after the first one or two, he really meant it, because he had seen me panic several times before and I had always bounced back, so he never doubted that with each subsequent experience, I could only improve (which I did, as will you).

I might put on some God-awful trashy TV for a little indulgence—on those occasions he certainly couldn't challenge me on my *Gilmore Girls* obsession—so I had my little victories on those crappy days too. I'd eat some nice comfort food and I'd call my mum, who always had nice reassuring things to say to me. You'll find that talking about it in a "yeah-this-happened," nonchalant kind of way is far more beneficial than pretending you are fine, which is massively counterproductive. I've never felt better for having bottled it up; in fact it would only worsen the feeling.

Having a few, key people who you can talk to about what's going on makes such a difference. As a rule, I'd then pour myself a bath and light every candle I could get my hands on. I'd add some essential oils to the water— check out my anxiety survival kit on in Chapter 8—and set a guided meditation on my Calm app so that I didn't have to do any work whatsoever "trying to meditate." I'd focus on nothing more than my breath, moving in and out, with some nice soothing sounds in the background. This was always the silver lining to my nimbus cloud of anxiety. I'd stay in the bath well beyond the point of pruning, before stepping into some hideously fluffy PJs, and climbing into bed with *Fifty Shades of Grey*, or something equally trivial, and a cup of chamomile tea. Finding something that makes you laugh after such an unnerving experience is a great reminder that you're doing just fine.

In those early, hard-to-understand days of my anxiety, when things were particularly bad, it took several days before I could shake the remnants of the panic attack from my body, and I got incredibly frustrated. I knew why it had happened, I could understand it and accept it, I knew how to take care of myself and I was doing just that, so why couldn't my body just hurry up and get over it? Yep, that didn't help either. After I experienced maybe five or six panic attacks, I just stood back and noticed a pattern. I always felt a bit ropey for the next one or two days, but when I knew this about myself, I learned to be okay with it, confident in the knowledge that, really soon, I'd feel like me again. I didn't need to put myself under pressure to be okay straightaway. Eventually, the recovery time got shorter, and then the time between these waves of panic got longer, until I reached a point where I rarely felt that kind of acute, debilitating anxiety.

But this is key, so please accept it. It wasn't being able to say to myself, "Oh, I haven't had a panic attack in four months, I must be doing well," that gave me confidence. This would be like saying, "I'm great as long as I don't have a panic attack." Instead, it was being able to say, "Meh, if I *do* have a panic attack, I can handle it." This is the secret, dear reader. It's simple, and it's one that can only be discovered through experience. Lucky for you, then, that you're having plenty of that.

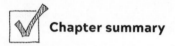 **Chapter summary**

- *Breathe.*

- *Let it happen to you.*

- *Know that it will pass.*

- *Have your own go-to comfort plan for when the physical feelings have passed.*

- *I appreciate that not everyone will want to share in the same way I do, but have your person who you can mention it to who won't say, "Oh My God," and freak you out even more. Don't try to pretend it didn't happen.*

- *Don't be upset with yourself; be really, really nice to yourself.*

- *Don't think that you're not getting anywhere. You are. Each panic attack is a learning experience.*

- *Focus on the comfort of the aftermath, which takes the fear out of the panic attack next time around.*

Exercise
EXERCISE: 5-4-3-2-1
GROUNDING EXERCISE

Grounding is a technique that helps us to reorient to the here and now, bringing us into the present. It is useful during a panic attack, or if you ever feel overwhelmed, intensely anxious, or dissociated from your environment.

The 5-4-3-2-1 game is a common, sensory-awareness, grounding exercise that many find a helpful tool to relax or get through difficult moments. These techniques work best if practiced regularly (every morning for example) for about three months. This helps to create the habit, as it is difficult to remember a grounding exercise in a moment of stress or panic if we are not used to doing them on a regular basis. Here it is:

1. Describe five things you see in the room.
2. Name four things you can feel ("my feet on the floor" or "the air in my nose").
3. Name three things you hear ("traffic outside").
4. Name two things you can smell (or two smells you like).
5. Name one good thing about yourself.

You should feel calmer and more at ease by the end of the exercise. Repeat the five steps more than once if you need to. Try out the technique in different situations; you may find it works well for insomnia, anxiety, or for general relaxation.

CHAPTER 7

Common mind traps associated with anxiety

IT'S VERY HELPFUL to be mindful of the various ways of thinking—and you'll definitely recognize these patterns in yourself—so that you can step back and realize when you've fallen into a "mind trap," often referred to as "cognitive distortions." The one I'm most guilty of? Catastrophizing, which we'll start with.

Catastrophizing

Catastrophizing is a distorted type of thinking that really amplifies anxiety. It's when we jump to the worst possible conclusion, expecting disaster, or we see something as being far worse than it actually is. Sound familiar? Jumping to the worst-case scenario is my super power.

We look at situations or challenges that face us, automatically imagining the worst possible thing that could happen.

Our minds continue this with the what-ifs game. This is when our minds go on and on: What if this worst-case scenario happens?

Catastrophizing can generally take two forms. In the first, it takes a current situation and gives it a truly negative "spin." The second occurs when we look to the future and anticipate all the things that are going to go wrong. Breaking the cycle can be hard, but as it is the case with anxiety overall there are some simple steps to acknowledge what's happening and stop it before it gets out of control:

- Recognize when you're doing it!

- Start recording your negative thoughts to yourself. Write down what happened and what you thought about the situation as objectively as you can, and then write down what your reaction or behaviors were.

- Change your self-talk to be more forgiving and "hopeful."

- Instead of trying to stop yourself from catastrophizing from here on out (it's a hard one to avoid), realize that the worst thing that "could" happen isn't always that terrible.

Polarized thinking

Polarized thinking happens when you believe that there are only right or wrong outcomes or views.

When you view things in terms of pure good or pure bad, it leads to unachievable standards and high stress levels.

Polarized thinking crops up when you find yourself basing your hopes and expectations on a single event or outcome, such as getting onto the college course you've dreamed about, wanting everyone to be impressed by you, a specific level of income or even a certain level of satisfaction.

- Realize that there are a lot of levels between triumph and tragedy, and that most things fall somewhere in between.

- Understand that no single accomplishment or failure is going to determine your future happiness.

- Don't expect that your values will never change or that other people will value the same things as you.

- Try to figure out what the actual consequences of failure are, and have a plan for dealing with those consequences.

Filtering

Filtering is taking the negative details and magnifying them while filtering out all positive aspects of a situation.

For example, a person may pick out a single, unpleasant detail and dwell on it exclusively, so that their vision of reality becomes darkened or distorted. This relates to the negativity bias which we discussed in Chapter 4.

- Learn to evaluate things clearly and objectively, even if you still feel more aware of the sh*t stuff.

- Look for positives.

- Resist "minimalizing" your efforts or achievements.

- Acknowledge your own growth by comparing how you have improved or done things better than a month/ year/five years ago.

Personalization

This is thinking that everything people do or say is some kind of reaction to you specifically. For example—and I've done this so many times—thinking that a friend's bad mood is because I've done something to irritate them, and so I search my mind for reasons to blame myself. You also compare yourself to others, trying to determine who's smarter, better-looking, etc.

The underlying assumption is that your worth is in question.

You are therefore continually forced to test your value as a person by measuring yourself against others. If you come out better, you get a moment's relief. If you come up short, you feel diminished. The basic thinking error is that you interpret each experience, each conversation, each look as a clue to your own worth and value.

- Understand that other people may not be aware that their bad moods are on display.

- Realize that others can have an awful lot going on in their heads.

- If you really think you've done something wrong—ask them.

- If nothing springs to mind, realize that you are most likely guilty of personalization, but don't berate yourself for it. Observe it.

- Try to avoid jumping to the conclusion that you are at fault next time around.

- Try not to change your behavior around the person; their mood is their issue.

Overgeneralizations

Overgeneralization is coming to a general conclusion based on a single incident or piece of evidence. If something bad happens once, we expect it to happen over and over again.

A person may see a single, unpleasant event as a never-ending pattern of defeat. Using "always" and "never" are clues that this style of thinking is at work.

This distortion can lead to a restricted life, as you avoid future failures based on the single incident or event. You jump to conclusions without individuals saying anything, as though you know what they are feeling and why they act the way they do. In particular, we are able to determine how people are feeling toward us. For example, a person may conclude that someone is reacting negatively toward them and don't actually bother to find out if they are correct. Another example is a person may anticipate that things will turn out badly, and will feel convinced that their prediction is already an established fact.

- Observe your tendency to overgeneralize in your day-to-day life.

- Next time, try to look at the facts; is it really "always" or "never" or are you dramatizing reality? Take your emotions out of it.

- Try to treat events in isolation, instead of taking things in the past as a predictor of what will happen in the future.

Attribution errors

Similar in ways to overgeneralizations, it's just crazy to believe you can correctly know a person's reasons for the way they behave. Their actions may or may not be deliberate.

The person may not even be aware of what they are doing (this is, in my experience, so often the case). Their actions may or may not be directed at you. Their actions may have unintended consequences or may result from an accident or chance.

We judge others based on behavior and we judge ourselves based on intent. It is difficult to determine cause when only the effect of something can be observed.

- Take heed of "consensus" information. If most people behave the same way when put in the same situation, then the situation is more likely to be the cause of the behavior.

- Ask yourself how you would behave in the same situation.

- Look for unseen causes, specifically looking for less-salient factors.

Simple steps to challenge unhelpful thinking

1. Be aware of what you are saying to yourself. Ask yourself: "What is going through my mind?" or "What is it about this situation that is upsetting me?"

2. Challenge your thoughts. Remember, just because you think something, doesn't mean it's true. Ask yourself: "Is this thought helpful?"; "Am I being realistic?"; "Would other people in this situation think these thoughts?"; "Is this an example of one of the common mind traps?"

3. Consider the following strategies and ask yourself some of these questions:

   - Look for evidence: What's the evidence for and against my thought? Am I focusing on the negatives and ignoring other information? Am I jumping to conclusions without looking at all the facts?

- Search for alternative explanations: Are there any other possible explanations? Is there another way of looking at this? Am I being too inflexible in my thinking?

- Put thoughts into perspective: Is it as bad as I am making out? What is the worst that could happen? How likely is it that the worst will happen? Even if it did happen, would it really be that bad? What could I do to get through it?

4. What is a more helpful thought? What can I say to myself that will help me remain calmer and help me achieve what I want to achieve in this situation?

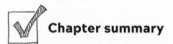 **Chapter summary**

- *Even if someone is not experiencing anxiety now, we all have the tendency to adopt these common mind traps in our day-to-day lives.*

- *It's really helpful to learn and be aware of these common mind traps, all of which can contribute toward feelings of anxiety.*

- *Observe which of these kinds of distorted thinking patterns you might regularly fall into. But as with everything else, don't beat yourself up about it.*

- *To become more familiar with mind traps, look for the same thing in other people—are your friends prone to overgeneralize and does that influence you?*

- *As much as you can, try to always bring everything back to objective facts.*

 Exercise
THOUGHT RECORD FOR MIND TRAPS

Negative thought:	Type of distortion:	Rational response:
For example, "I'm never not going to feel anxious."	Catastrophic thinking	"I feel anxious now but I won't always feel this way. I am doing the necessary work to help myself."

CHAPTER
6

Anxiety survival kit

IN NO PARTICULAR order, the following is a list of things to do and things that I keep at home (and in my handbag too) for when I'm feeling a little stressed or sense that a bout of anxiety might be on the horizon. They won't yield any major or life-changing results (that's what the other chapters are for) but they will help to soothe your mind and body in the moment, and the more time we spend focusing on doing that, the better.

1. Drink up (herbal tea, not booze)
2. Sleep well
3. Start an essential oil collection
4. Spend time with animals
5. Download some meditation apps
6. Create a calm living space
7. Stock up on stationery

8. Have a bath
9. Allow yourself some worry time
10. Make an instant-calm playlist
11. Create a Pinterest board of your favorite quotes
12. Have a few key books that you enjoy on your nightstand
13. Get out into nature
14. Find your person
15. Find a feel-good hobby

Drink up (herbal tea, not booze)

Have a cup of herbal tea, and make sure it's caffeine-free.

Below are my favorite herbal teas that promote feelings of relaxation, but a comforting cup of hot water, lemon and honey can sometimes do the trick. For something relaxing *and* immune-boosting, I reach for a cup of bone broth:

- Lavender
- Chamomile
- Lemon balm
- Valerian root
- Green tea (This has caffeine in it, which is normally a no-go for anxiety, but it also has the very soothing L-theanine, which cancels out the stimulatory effect on your body; go for matcha if you're into it.)

Sleep well

As we'll explore in Chapter 15, sleep is essential for the management of anxiety. My essential, quick-fix, go-to sleep aid is: This Works Sleep Pillow Spray. I'm never without it, and advise you order it online if you can't get it in a store nearby. Even if I'm really struggling to quiet my mind, the scent alone is soothing.

Start an essential oil collection

Essential oils are great for calming anxiety. Ideally, you'll have a nice bath and add a few drops of your chosen oil to the water. But if you have to go out, you can also use the oil topically by dabbing it on your pulse points. If you have a friend or family member with magic hands, an at-home massage is another great use for essential oils; or if your time and budget allow go out for a professional rub-down. My favorite oils are:

- Neroli oil
- Lavender oil
- Vetiver oil
- Chamomile oil
- Bergamot oil
- Frankincense

Spend time with animals

Looking into the eyes of a dog is said to increase oxytocin in humans, a feel-good hormone that will counteract feelings of anxiety. Pets are always a good idea, unless you're scared of dogs or allergic to cats, etc., in which case skip this one.

Download some meditation apps

Knowing you have a helping voice in your phone is always a reassuring comfort. I've found the following to be particularly helpful:

- Headspace
- Calm
- Stop, Breathe & Think

Create a calm living space

I always feel better when I'm happy in my home environment, and a cozy space—even if it's just your bedroom—where you feel at ease, will help to calm you. Keep clutter to a minimum, prioritize soft, soothing lighting and make sure it's a place you want to spend time. Make it your safe space.

Stock up on stationery

For all of your exercises, gratitude diary entries, to-do lists and even just for some distracting doodling, it's all the more enjoyable and calming when you've got some nice notebooks to write in. You feel empowered, in control and on top of things (well, I certainly do).

Have a bath

Utilize all of the accoutrements that make a bath more enjoyable. You need candles, maybe an indulgent bath bomb, a nice playlist on your speaker, and you need the bathroom to be clean. Make use of your essential oils here too. You can also practice your breathing exercises in the bath. Make sure the water temperature is just right—too often, I've endured baths that are too hot, making my heart race faster than feels comfortable. This sometimes exacerbates feelings of anxiety so if you feel worse after the bath, it's probably because it was too hot.

Allow yourself some worry time

We spend so much of our time punishing ourselves for worrying or analyzing, especially when trying to get a grip on our anxiety. We read about mindfulness and then berate ourselves when our minds wander off somewhere negative. It's hard to avoid worrying—so don't. Instead, schedule time for it. Give yourself ten minutes each day to let your mind run free with any worries, big or small. The next time you feel like fretting, you can compartmentalize, telling yourself that you don't need to worry about that now because you can do it during your designated worry time. Then when it's time for your planned worry session, you'll be less likely to think catastrophically.

Make an instant-calm playlist

This could be really upbeat pop music if that's what makes you feel good, but I always find listening to slower, soothing music has an instantly soothing effect on my mind and body. I particularly like to listen to older music from the likes of Billie Holiday or Ella Fitzgerald.

If you're looking for inspiration, Spotify has plenty of playlists that have been expertly collated to induce feelings of calm. They will definitely have a more positive effect on you than heavy dance music, which is far more stimulating.

Create a Pinterest board of your favorite quotes

Yes, a lot of what you find there can be total BS, but you will find a sentiment or two that will really speak to you. Seeing them laid out in a way that's aesthetically pleasing helps the message to register—and you spend time enjoying it. This is also just a very reassuring exercise that you can always go back to when you need a little bit of encouragement.

Have a few key books that you enjoy on your nightstand

Some might be fiction, one might be this one you're reading, but it's always a comfort to have hard copy books to hand in case you ever need to curl up and remind yourself that we're all in this together. For me, it doesn't get better than Elizabeth Gilbert or Brené Brown. Reading also relaxes the mind (unless you're reading a nail-biting thriller, which I would just avoid in times of acute anxiety), more so than TV or screen-time which would be stimulating.

Get out into nature

When I was at my worst, someone told me to stand barefoot in the grass. Now, this isn't always practical but it's a very literal way of grounding yourself and, like it or not, the healing powers of nature cannot be denied. It's just good for you. Do you ever feel bad after a nice stroll with some soothing music in your ear? If you can manage it, get to the beach; the air and the views will have a very positive effect—even if it's just temporarily.

Find your person

I explore this more in Chapter 13, but as we're social creatures by nature, one of the easiest ways to feel better is to connect with someone that you trust. It doesn't mean you need to unload all of your stress onto them and drag them down, but being able to tell someone that you're not feeling so great and that you could do with the company—without having to perform or pretend like you're good—is hugely helpful.

In this instance, you're better off briefly addressing how you're feeling and then engaging in something that makes you feel good to refocus your attention. Maybe that's having a good bitch about what your frenemies have been up to on Facebook—it can be whatever tickles your fancy.

Find a feel-good hobby

For you, it might be mindful coloring or reorganizing your wardrobe or even knitting, which has become popular all over again on account of how collectively stressed out we are and how delightfully soothing an activity it can be. Physically distracting your mind—not just to avoid the feeling—helps to lessen anxiety.

CHAPTER 9

BS-free inspirational quotes and affirmations

A LOT OF the affirmations or "inspirational quotations" you're likely to find on social media would absolutely fall under the category of bullsh*t and therefore don't feature in this book. Some of what you'll read sure sounds pretty—especially when scrolled in some vintage, hipster font—but, when you break it down, it barely makes any sense. More often than not, you'll find yourself rolling your eyes at some of the stuff people share on social media.

Having said all that, how I feel about inspirational words mirrors how I feel about horoscopes: If you get something out of it, that's all that matters (even if it is all BS). It may be a line of poetry, the profundity of which stops you in your tracks, or it may be something that sounds philosophical but was actually just created by a greeting card company to make money. If something resonates with you and makes you feel good, I don't care what it is (well, within reason of course), and neither should you.

Inspirational quotations will definitely read as BS to someone who isn't looking for something with which they can connect—but that's because they don't need it. The same goes for someone who's blissfully happy and doesn't desperately need to find some kind of meaning or reassurance from their horoscope. Some day soon, you won't either. But if, right now, you're feeling down, anxious, depressed, sad, lonely, frustrated—anything along those lines—such words can envelope you like a hug, giving you an injection of comfort when you need it. So in that regard, I don't see them as bullsh*t. Granted, a string of quotations alone won't help you overcome your anxiety, but, together with everything else you're doing, they can't hurt.

Below are some of the quotations that appeal to me, words that I'll always go back to. They mightn't do it for you, but you'll find yours.

"Let your faith be bigger than your fear."
—Anonymous

My fear and anxiety were pretty big but if my faith that I will be okay eventually is just the tiniest bit bigger than the fear itself, I'll come out on top. I don't think of the word "faith" here in any religious sense, but just in terms of having the belief in yourself to pull through.

"What if I fall? Oh, my darling, what if you fly?"

—Erin Hanson

It sounds poetic but this is a question I have to ask myself any time I feel unsure or when my anxiety is holding me back from something that would do me good. I like to think of this as a conversation between the part of you that's scared and your higher self who knows you'll be okay. Having this kind of dialogue with yourself is helpful, you just have to dig deep to find the voice that's confident, it's always in there somewhere.

I often look to my favorite book, *Eat Pray Love* by Elizabeth Gilbert, for pearls of wisdom. The section I find myself returning to most often is one where the author is experiencing a night of despair and writes a letter to herself. It's a piece of writing I read and re-read (and re-read again) when I feel I need to find that voice inside me that says "Hey, it's okay." It's less a quote and more an entire passage, so my advice to you is to give it the attention it deserves.

On these pages, Elizabeth Gilbert splits herself in two—there's the struggling, anxious, lonely, depressed part of herself who seems to be the one in the driving seat, and there's the quietly confident inner self who has got her back. The part of her who offers her all of the certainties she's always wished that another person would say when she's feeling troubled. When she feels that all hope is lost, and she finally accepts the presence of these unhelpful emotions in the here and now, the stronger, higher self emerges from deep within to remind her that whatever happens, she's going to be okay. She also turns loneliness and depression into characters to great effect, which can sometimes be helpful when it comes to anxiety too. She takes pen to paper and allows this reassuring voice to run free. *I'm here, I love you*, it tells her. It will stay with her if she has to cry all night long. It's stronger than the feelings of anxiety, loneliness or depression, and it can never be exhausted.

At first, it might sound a bit tree-huggery, but this idea of self-love and self-reliance is so important. There really is a part of you that can never be exhausted, and by reminding yourself of that, or even starting to practice writing or thinking with this strong internal voice, you will feel stronger bit by bit. For Elizabeth Gilbert, finding that inner strength was only possible after reaching what felt like her emotional rock-bottom. It was a similar, but a far less poetic experience for me. My "voice" emerged in the middle of the night, right in the middle of my worst anxiety. I said to myself, and then to my boyfriend, "No. This is not how things are going to be for me. I'm going to get on top of this, I'm stronger than I know, and I'm going to write a book about it one day and it's going to be *brilliant*." You'll be the judge of the latter.

> **"What screws us up most in life is the picture in our head of how it's supposed to be."**—*Anonymous*

Yep. That's a precursor to anxiety right there.

> **"When something goes wrong in your life, just yell, 'PLOT TWIST!' and move on."**—*Molly Weis*

We didn't plan things this way, but it's happened now, so we'll have to deal with it. As I repeat about four hundred times throughout this book, we've got to accept what has happened and move forward.

> **"It is not uncommon for people to spend their whole life waiting to start living."**
>
> —*Eckhart Tolle*, The Power of Now

You *are* living. Even with anxiety.

> **"Be where you are, not where you think you should be."**—*Anonymous*

Another take on acceptance.

> **"Nothing is permanent in this wicked world, not even our troubles."**—*Charlie Chaplin*

Even if things feel like utter sh*t, you are still here, getting through it. Good for you.

"Have patience with all things, but first of all, with yourself."—*Saint Francis de Sales*

Practice patience; just as Diana Ross said you can't hurry love, you also can't rush into wellness.

"Life is tough, my darling, but so are you."
—*Stephanie Bennett-Henry*

Spend as much time as you can believing that you're stronger than your anxiety makes you feel.

"Accept—then act. Whatever the present moment contains, accept it as if you had chosen it. Always work with it, not against it. Make it your friend and ally, not your enemy. This will miraculously trans-form your whole life."—*Eckhart Tolle*

A man after my own heart, so yep, I'll quote him twice.

"A diamond is merely a lump of coal that did well under pressure."—*Henry Kissinger*

I've always felt strongly about this. As Nietzsche put it, that which does not kill you makes you stronger, and so on and so forth.

> **"People often say that motivation doesn't last.
> Well, neither does bathing—that's why we
> recommend it daily."**
>
> *—Zig Ziglar, American author and motivational speaker*

This quotation reminds me of the fact that wellness is a linear progression; we have to keep it up each day and deal with the ebb and flow of life.

And to finish: *F*ck it*, which is just from me.

Write your five favorite quotations—whoever said them, even Winnie the Pooh—into your designated *Own It* journal, and revisit them whenever you feel the need.

If you want to go one step further, create your own list of affirmations. Dr. Coyne explains:

> Using positive affirmations can be really helpful in building up our psychological immune systems, which we can later employ in times of stress. New research has found that self-affirmation can protect against the damaging effects of stress on problem-solving performance. The process of identifying and focusing on one's most important values has been found to boost individuals' problem-solving abilities while under stress.
>
> While "I" statements can work for some, if you don't believe what you are saying, they can actually backfire. A more promising approach may be to engage in "self-affirmation" exercises, such as writing about the things you most value in your life. This can have a significant positive impact on

your psychological well-being and your feelings of self-worth and can also help you to respond more constructively to anxiety-related threats, as you are engaging the power of your prefrontal cortex over your amygdala.

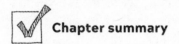 **Chapter summary**

- *If inspirational quotations help you, by all means, indulge.*

- *Affirmations and quotations give you a chance to pause and think and they're usually quite comforting and encouraging.*

- *If you get nothing from them, that's okay, too.*

PART TWO

Addressing Anxiety

Acceptance is key

YOU ARE HERE, in this present moment, at this present time and, whatever reason (or set of reasons) brought you here, you cannot press a magical rewind button. You also don't live in a world where those memory erasers from *Men in Black* exist (if only, right?). When we feel anxious or distressed, we naturally obsess over the future and we dwell negatively on the past. Either that, or we look back on earlier times with rose-colored glasses, believing that everything seemed just peachy keen and we hadn't a care in the world. Now, I'm not about to tell you to simply stop thinking about the past and stop worrying about the future—nor would I suggest that you try a staring competition with a tree because if you stare long enough and hard enough, their grounded, rooted wisdom will inevitably impart itself onto you—no, that would be bullsh*t and you'd rightly want to chuck this book in the trash.

But, bear with me. What I do urge is that you accept your situation (I know, I say it a lot, but it's *the* most important thing). Don't "try" to do anything, don't "try" really hard to just feel different or have a self-induced personality transplant, just . . . accept.

I know you feel like a sack of garbage right now, and you'd do anything to run a million miles from yourself if only to feel even the tiniest bit better, but you can't. And resistance to that fact will only worsen your situation. I also know that it's frustrating and hard to accept a situation that you don't want to be in. As for embracing it? Forget it.

But that's the crux of this whole thing; our perception of it, our acceptance of it, and our eventual ability to embrace it.

After my first whopper meltdown—when I started bawling uncontrollably into my bowl of ramen, in the midst of what felt like an earth-shattering, out-of-nowhere panic attack—I gave myself such a fright that I instantly developed a crippling fear of the anxiety symptoms themselves. I wasn't afraid of what might happen to me—some people fear that a panic attack will give them a heart attack. I was afraid of the feeling of fear. I had a fear of the fear, if you will.

To non-anxious people that sounded ridiculous. Surely if you're just afraid of being afraid you can just stop being afraid because you're not actually afraid of anything other than fear. But it's not that easy; I couldn't fool myself. All of those symptoms—trembling hands, racing heart, adrenaline coursing through my body, I even had sore gums from clenching my teeth so tightly—felt harmful, even though it was anxiety and nothing more sinister. But the fact that my state of mind could induce such a physical reaction was sinister enough for me. Give me the demon from *Paranormal Activity* any day, just don't leave me in the company of my own destructive thoughts.

For an intense period of time after that first incident, I lived my life from one anxiety attack to the next, afraid to mention it in calmer moments in case I brought it on, and crumbling to the floor if it did take hold of me. In fact, I kind of *did* think of it as a horror movie demon or some source of negative energy that decided when it wanted to rule the roost.

At the time, I was living in an apartment and to get to the nearest shop, I had to drive past a mental health hospital. My biggest fear up to that point had been the idea of a meteor crashing into the Earth, but it was swiftly trumped by my fear of winding up in a mental health institution, having "thought" myself to the point of no return. I smile at that thought now, but, God, it was such a powerful visualization at the time that it brought me out in hives—I drove many an unnecessarily long journey to avoid passing the hospital for fear I'd "catch" some kind of contagious psychosis.

Whenever I felt the slightest hint of anxiety—physically—I'd lose it, even if I wasn't feeling particularly troubled by anything. "Well, that's it, I'm freaking out, I must be really anxious about something because my heart is pounding and I'm feeling antsy for no apparent reason so obviously I must just be f*cking crazy. Send for the men in white coats, go on, I'm done, I give up."

Sound familiar?

But that was a very unhelpful and destructive perception of my stress response. And while psychologists and health professionals have, for years, been warning about the damage that stress (and we know that anxiety is just a more extreme form of stress) can inflict on our bodies, compelling new research suggests that it's not necessarily the fault of the stress or anxiety in themselves; it's because we've been conditioned to perceive those feelings and symptoms as something really bad. The enemy. The demon. Something to run away from.

When I was introduced to Stanford psychologist Kelly McGonigal's incredible work, I had a breakthrough. Instead of trying to avoid stress (because that doesn't work) and miraculously rid my mind and body of the ability to feel anxious (highly unlikely despite the number of books that say otherwise), what if I worked on my perceptions of it? That is something I could feasibly do, with practice, experience and the right information.

First, I had to accept the inevitability of stress and anxiety (a handy shortcut through the unnecessary turmoil of trying to dodge it all through your life). Then, I had to accept my own body's sensitivity and that I'm just one of those people who feels everything to the extreme, which is both a blessing (remember the less sh*t side to anxiety?) and a curse. Though I may have wished it, I couldn't crawl back into my mother's womb and start over, emerging this time around with a suit of indestructible armor. This was me, warts and all (for the record, I have no warts).

Next, I had to look at my symptoms and work on my perceptions of them. Instead of treating myself and my body's reaction to stress as the enemy, I cultivated a frame of mind in which I took a much softer approach, looking at my body as an overeager and concerned parent. As for the racing heart and the trembling limbs? That's not me falling apart or me not coping, that's my body preparing me for a challenge and enabling me to cope. What it most certainly is not is a sign that I *cannot* cope.

So, you're probably saying to yourself, "Okay, so what if I convince myself it's not the worst thing in the world, I still feel like crap." That's where the research comes in handy.

When you change your mind about stress or anxiety, you change your body's response to it, thus reducing the symptoms. When you accept your feelings of anxiety and stop looking at them as your one-way ticket to crazy town, your body actually believes you, and your stress response becomes healthier.

But don't just take my word for it. In McGonigal's TED Talk, "How To Make Stress Your Friend" (bookmark that sh*t *now*), she cites a number of key studies that help you rethink your perceptions of stress and anxiety.

One particular study chronicled 30,000 adults in the U.S. over an eight-year period. All the participants were asked how much stress they'd experienced in the previous year, as well as whether or not they believed that stress was harmful for their health. Then, rather grimly, the researchers used public death records to find out who'd kicked the bucket. People who had experienced a huge amount of stress the previous year had a 43 percent increased chance of dying. But don't freak out yet because that was only true for the people who also believed that stress was a terrible affliction. People who'd experienced a lot of stress but *didn't* think it was harmful were even less likely to die than those who'd experienced little to no stress at all. That's got to mean something, right?

As explained by McGonigal, how you think and feel about stress actually matters more than the presence of stress in your body; she says, "When you choose to view your stress response as helpful, you create the biology of courage and confidence."

What's more, she suggests, feeling stressed out or anxious should be viewed as something that just gives us more experience, and makes us better at dealing with future stress and anxiety. While McGonigal hones in on particularly stressful activities—for example, if you have to stand up in front of a room of people and give a speech (excuse me while I vomit)—I would majorly advocate that adapting your perceptions and accepting the presence of stress and anxiety in general will vastly improve your experience of it overall, not just during isolated moments of increased pressure.

Start practicing your acceptance now, interrupt any negative perceptions and thoughts and replace them with more accurate and helpful perceptions.

Here, you'll find some examples of my own former perceptions (those that were not helpful and served only to perpetuate the anxiety) versus how I perceive any feelings of anxiety today, which really, truly, diminishes the nastiness.

"Oh sh*t, I'm really anxious." "I'm feeling a bit anxious, that's okay."

"I hate my anxiety, f*ck this sh*t." "Now, Caroline, anxiety is not the enemy, you are not possessed, your body's just trying to protect you."

"My hands are trembling, sh*t, sh*t, sh*t! I'm losing it."

 VS

"My body thinks I need an extra spurt of adrenaline right now. I don't, but eventually it will learn not to jump the gun. This trembling feeling will go away."

"My life is over, this is not a way to live. I am f*cked."

VS

"Granted, I'm feeling pretty crap right now, but physically I understand what's happening in my body and I also know that it's temporary. All feelings, good and bad, are transient."

"I can't do all of these things that I have to do!"

VS

"The physical symptoms of anxiety are making me think that I'll never be able to cope but: (a) these thoughts will settle down when the physical symptoms settle down; and (b) these symptoms are here to help me to cope and get me through."

"If I don't overcome this anxiety it will ruin my future." "I'm getting really good experience of anxiety, I'm going to get really good at managing it and, in the future, I'll know exactly how to dissolve any sh*tty feelings if they arise."

"I'm the only person who has anxiety this bad." "Every single person has experienced or will experience anxiety—just ask around—and because I'm dealing with this now, I'm going to be even more equipped to deal with anything the future might throw at me."

"I am so scared, what if I never improve?" VS "I feel scared but my faith in myself is bigger than my fear."

Finally, don't go beating yourself up if your thoughts and perceptions fall mostly within the first column; mine did.

How were we to know? That's a totally natural reaction and one that you've long been conditioned to have, but now that you're addressing and reconsidering things head on, you'll begin to reap the benefits.

 **Chapter summary**

- *Every time you find yourself dwelling on past experiences, stop. Focus on how to make yourself feel good in the here and now.*

- *Remember, it's our perception of stress and anxiety that really makes the difference to our experience of both.*

- *Instead of trying to get rid of anxiety, which is just a waste of energy, focus on changing your perception of it. Your body's got your back.*

- *A change in attitude toward anxiety will also have a tangible effect on the physical effects of the anxiety itself.*

- *Face the fear of the fear itself head on and accept that anxiety is a totally normal bodily function.*

- *When you feel a bad bout of anxiety coming on, just let it happen. Say to yourself that it's okay, reaffirm that you accept that you feel anxious, and it will start to dissipate.*

- *When you don't feel anxious, don't take false comfort in the idea that you're "cured." The fact is you'll probably feel anxious again at some point and that's okay, we all do. It's the desperately trying to avoid a recurrence that will bring it on ten times worse. Again, let it be. Listen to some John Lennon if it helps.*

CHAPTER
11

Know the difference between personality and anxiety

IT'S FAIR TO say that most people who are dealing with anxiety are very hard on themselves. If you had a gentler and more understanding approach—which together we will cultivate—you would be less likely to get so frustrated, thus reducing your anxiety. What's really important here is the ability to distinguish clearly between your anxiety and your personality, that thing that defines you. This is particularly relevant when it comes to making decisions but it can take a while to spot the difference and it's a hard one to explain. Let's try, though, shall we?

One of the biggest roadblocks for me in getting to a point of owning and reducing my anxiety was the need to please others. This is something that most people can relate to; we all want to be liked, we all want to fit in, we all want to be included, and it's only as we really begin to mature that we stop—if at all—and say to ourselves, "Hold on, do I actually *want* to do that?"

For so long, I felt that if I didn't go at the same pace as my peers, I'd fall behind or be left out or seem like I was uncool or no fun. (I know, you'd think all of that would stop after your early teens but it really doesn't. I'm holding out for my thirties.) And as is also the case for most people, this pressure was coming mostly from within. When choosing whether or not to do something, I blamed all sense of unease on my anxiety, never stopping to say, "Well maybe, regardless of my anxiety, I'm just not that into it."

I really pushed myself into doing things that were never going to fit well with me as a person, and that was massively counterproductive. It just made me feel more anxious. The thing is, though, there's a fine line between managing your anxiety so that it doesn't manage you and doing things that just don't sit right with you. It's really so important that, for the most part, we aim to suit our personalities and do what makes us happy without feeling bad about it. For example, if you just hate the thought of slumming it at a five-day music festival while your best friends think it sounds like heaven, don't force yourself to feel the way they do. Book a day ticket. Book a hotel. Do what *you* need to do to suit yourself, and don't make any apologies for prioritizing what makes you feel good.

> **When you face a situation that makes you feel uneasy, simply ask yourself this question: "If you could switch off your anxiety entirely, would you still want to go through with whatever it was?" If the answer to this is no, then it's probably your personality talking. That's you. And that's who you should listen to and be nice to and give a break to and stop trying to change. To me, it makes sense that if you keep doing things that don't make you feel good, you won't feel very good (greetings, Captain Obvious at your service). If, however, you find yourself saying, "I wish I could do that but I'm scared," then it's more than likely that your anxiety is holding you back and you absolutely should work toward pushing through that fear.**

It's a fairly simple formula when you think about it: Spend more time pleasing others and less time pleasing yourself and you'll stoke the fires of your anxiety. Accept and embrace the person you are, do what makes you happy without feeling bad about it and you will, without doubt, reduce your anxiety.

When I eventually decided to say, "You know what? I have absolutely no interest in jumping out of a plane and that's okay," life got a whole lot easier. (Thanks, also, in large part to *The Life-Changing Magic of Not Giving a*

F**k by Sarah Knight, which I highly recommend. In it, she teaches us how to do what makes us happy instead of always doing what will make others happy, while at the same time managing our time so as not to be totally selfish or potentially hurtful to others.)

Today, there are plenty of situations where my personality will reign supreme. For one, I've always enjoyed music festivals—but I have a long, enduring love affair with my own bed. I want to go to the festival, dance, have fun, have my face painted, take selfies of said face paint and then, when I've had enough, I want to go home and have a hot shower, before slipping into my PJs and my beloved place of slumber. The idea of staying put for a full weekend at a remote camping ground, wading through the mud and shivering the night away is just not my own personal idea of a good time. For some people, it doesn't get better, and I salute that, but I've always been a creature of comforts, and it's just not in my DNA to get excited about the idea of a barefoot jungle trek. I don't care how much fresh air you might be getting.

In my teens and early twenties, I was never that keen on traveling, mainly because I was afraid of feeling anxious away from home, not because I had zero interest in what lies beyond my hometown. I really wanted to see the world, I just wanted to feel good doing it. In this case, I knew it was my anxiety making the decision to hold back; I knew that if I could remove all feelings of fear from my mind and body, I'd already be sipping a piña colada on some far-flung island. Today, I still might feel a bit anxious about traveling, but I know that I want to do it. What's more, I know that by not doing it, I would be doing myself a disservice.

A simple example of where my personality eventually reigned supreme might be me in my late teens versus me now. Back then, when I went out with friends, it was almost a contest to see who'd be the last man standing at the end of the night. Getting messy was the goal because it meant you had a story to tell the following day; it meant you were carefree and fun. There were so many times that I felt under pressure to stay out until the sun came up because I was afraid of seeming boring. And this pressure was coming from me, nobody else.

My response today? "F*ck it."

I go out when I want to go out, I stay out as long as I want to stay out (sometimes it *is* 6 AM), and when I'm out I have a *lot* of fun. And I only drink as much alcohol as suits me (which, for my sensitive body, is usually relatively little). When I get tired or stop having fun, I go home to my bed—preferably with a six-pack box of chicken nuggets from McDonalds that are not for sharing—and that is what makes me happy.

Going home at 2 AM instead of 4 AM doesn't mean I've had less of a good time, nor does it mean that I'm less of a fun person, but—and here's the key—making a decision like that is not something I do to suit my anxiety, it's to suit my personality, which, in turn, makes me feel less anxious in general.

It's of paramount importance that we spend more time focusing on what makes us happy and doing less of what doesn't. If you've been suffering with anxiety, perhaps it's time to put yourself first for a change. More pertinently, it's time to prioritize nurturing activities over the things that deplete our energy (and/or contribute to our anxiety).

Try this exercise to see how much of your time you're spending pleasing others instead of yourself.

Chapter summary

- *Your anxiety doesn't define you; your personality does.*

- *Just because you are experiencing anxiety now, it is not part of who you are forever.*

- *It's really important to know the difference between challenging your anxiety, so that you can overcome it, and pushing yourself into situations that don't bode well with you.*

- *Don't be afraid to say no to anything that's going to exacerbate your anxiety. You don't always have to push yourself.*

- *You don't have to go at the same pace as everyone around you—just do you.*

- *If you know that you would like to do something but fear it's your anxiety holding you back, then this is precisely the kind of thing you should try to confront.*

- *Watch out for too many depleting activities; prioritize nourishing ones instead.*

Exercise
NOURISHING VS. DEPLETING ACTIVITIES

Do you ever find that, when you feel stressed or low, you are more likely to look at life through "gloomy specs" and see everything through a negative filter? You may also neglect the nourishing activities that help you to feel better. Many of us stop doing the things we enjoy and only do the things we really have to do, which can further deplete us. We might end up doing very little, which isolates us from loved ones and often makes us feel worse.

One very effective way to realign the way we live our lives is to create an action plan to maintain our emotional well-being through engaging in nourishing activities. Just the ability to stop and pay attention to the emotional impact of our daily activities enables us to see what needs to be taken care of in our lives.

Step 1

In two columns, write lists of your normal daily activities in:

- A typical work / weekday; and
- A typical day off / weekend day.

Be sure to include everything you can think of, including getting up, showering, getting dressed, eating breakfast, washing the dishes, activities with children, etc.

In the last rows, expand your list to include things you do once a week or once a year. The goal is to get a good mix of activities that represent how you spend your time.

Step 2

When you have completed the above daily activities lists, decide how each activity affects your mood and energy levels and write either N, D or O next to each activity.

- N for those activities that **nourish** you, i.e., lift your mood, increase your energy, help you feel calm, and increase your sense of being alive and present rather than merely existing.
- D for those activities that **deplete** you, i.e., lower your mood, drain your energy, increase your stress and tension and decrease your sense of being alive and present.
- O for anything **neutral**, i.e., neither nourishing nor depleting.

Step 3

You have now created a mind map where you can see at a glance the balance of your life. Are there too many depleting activities? Is your life overly busy with activities that bring you down? Are there enough nourishing activities to counteract the depleting ones?

You can gain a healthier balance of activities and build positive experiences by:

- Increasing the number of nourishing activities: What will you do differently? When? How? With whom?
- Reducing or making changes to the depleting activities: What will you do differently? When? How? With whom?
- Changing the meaning of those depleting activities you can't avoid doing: Is there another way to look at this? Can you bring nourishment to these activities?

Why social comparison is bad for you

THE NEXT VITAL step toward owning your anxiety is this—stop comparing yourself to others. I know, easier said than done, but this is one of the most dominant culprits behind your suffering.

Unfortunately, the act of social comparison—or "keeping up with the Joneses"—is deeply ingrained in all of us. Why? Well, according to Leon Festinger, the psychologist behind Social Comparison Theory, we do this in an attempt make accurate evaluations about ourselves. We determine our own social and personal worth based on how we stack up against others. A healthy dose of comparison and awareness of others can and should be motivating—it can drive us to succeed, grow and improve—the thing is, there's a very fine line between being spurred on by those around you and winding up in a perpetual cycle of self-doubt.

Much like your old pal the negativity bias, it's one of those innate human functions that is supposed to help us, but, in today's modern world, it's more of an evolutionary pain in the ass, and one that's fraught with unnecessary anguish. Festinger even goes so far as to say that our desire to compare ourselves to others is almost as powerful as our drive for thirst or hunger, hence it's a habit we cannot ignore on the road to owning our anxiety.

The good news, however, is that, with time, it's yet another thing we can consciously step back from and rewire.

So why is it bad for us?

Besides that deflated, crap feeling you'll be familiar with after a social media binge, on a more long-term basis, this kind of comparison actually encourages us to devalue our own sense of worth. And if we rely on social comparison to consistently evaluate our self-worth, we're choosing to enter a battle that we cannot win. What's more, the information we use to compare ourselves to others is, thanks to social media, more skewed and inaccurate than ever. While social comparison can be informative, it's heavily tinged with discouragement, because whatever way it works out, someone's always going to end up on the bottom.

These days, it seems that we are beginning to wise up to the fact that what you see on social media is always a highly edited version of reality; it's the best bits, the highlights reel—and far from the whole truth. While I believe we know this, it can still have a very tangible and negative effect on us. Even more so if you're already feeling sensitive or vulnerable. Picture this: You've had a bad day at school or work, and you're lying in bed (Desitin dotted all over your face as is often my norm) scrolling habitually through all of your social media newsfeeds on a "liking" frenzy. You click "like" while in your head you're thinking, "I wish that was me" or "I could never do that" or even "theirs is bigger."

From what you can see, your peers are having one hell of an amazing life, achieving their goals and looking great—even their dinner looks better than yours! While, at first, you just felt a bit below par about your own day, you're now acutely aware of how "amazing" it's been for everyone else. Your own crappy day becomes magnified. Tenfold. Well, dear reader, this is just more bullsh*t.

Despite the obvious perils that we've all felt, we still can't resist the urge to binge on other people's best bits—several times a day—or worse still, enter social media stalking mode with someone whom we either admire or are envious of, engaging in a destructive, them-versus-us exercise, from which nothing good can come. I've certainly never found it to be a rewarding activity, have you?

Social media certainly added a whole heap of fuel to my own anxious fire—in fact, it was like a renewable energy source that would have been better utilized to power a city. When my anxiety reached its apex, I made a decision to just retreat from it entirely. As I was already very fragile and considerably depressed (the depression was, for me, a consequence of the prolonged anxiety), it was bringing me nothing but added misery. I didn't enjoy seeing all the fun stuff that everyone else was up to; it was akin to having someone stand there with a megaphone, reminding me every five minutes about just how much I was floundering. I wanted to spend more time doing things that made me forget to check my phone.

As explained in a 1998 study in the *Clinical Psychology Review*, under certain circumstances, this kind of self-comparison can be very damaging and serve only as an application to enhance or bring about feelings of depression and anxiety.

I already had enough anxiety to be dealing with, thank you very much. I had to give myself a break, accept that I was where I was, and that the last thing I needed was the added pressure of social media telling me that I was falling behind everyone else. Though it sounds trivial now, I actually felt worse because I felt I had nothing interesting to say on my own social media. I felt irrelevant. While others' statuses read: "Day one, world tour, first stop Bali," mine would have read: "Day twenty, sitting in my living room yet again, too afraid to leave the house." There was no way I was going to expose myself like that. Instead, I chose to take a timeout. It was *so* necessary. The sky didn't fall down in the absence of any mind-blowing social updates and, finally, I felt I had the space to breathe, away from the smoke and mirrors of social media. I had the headspace to focus on myself alone.

Only when I stopped engaging in social media and stopped observing the seemingly wonderful lives of others did I realize how damaging an activity it was (and still is). Not only was I caught in the habit of negative self-comparison, from which nothing good could come, I also realized how much we rely on social media for gratification, and how, in the absence of this gratification (or "likes"), our sense of self-worth could often nosedive, while our anxiety would often rise to the surface.

You'll recognize this in yourself. For example, you share a tweet that you think is pure comedy gold. You refresh your feed obsessively to see who's picked it up. You get one, maybe two likes at best. No retweets. No replies. And you're filled with doubt and anxiety. You might even go back to Twitter and just delete it. It affects us, negatively. Equally, it's just as concerning that I'd get a noticeable confidence boost after sharing something that garnered a positive reaction from friends and followers. This is something that, again, we're all familiar with; racking up the "likes" is like a badge of honor, we equate it with popularity and we rely on popularity as another determining factor of our self-worth. While it makes us feel good for a few moments, it's a fleeting, meaningless feeling that can just as easily go the other way when you post something that doesn't wow the masses, and you feel as if you're not good enough. It's more than a little bit messed up that we would turn to technology and the approval of random acquaintances to determine our self-worth, don't you think?

When it comes to looking after your mental health, just be wary; social media is an innocent-looking minefield, and one that should be entered with caution.

Today, while I probably engage with social media more than ever, I try to do so with awareness. I know that most of it is pure bullsh*t and I don't take anything too seriously. I use it as a tool for getting my news, watching videos of newborn puppies and keeping up with my friends' antics. But if I really want to connect with a friend, on a more meaningful level—and one that will actually bring me joy—I'll pick up the phone or make a plan to see them in person. When I find myself falling into that cycle of scrolling and realizing that my mood has started to descend, I gently pull myself out of it. But, again, it's important here not to get mad at yourself for doing it. Observe and refocus your attention toward the positive.

Understanding the negative effects of social comparison—especially on social media—helps me to step back and realize what's happening. In the same way, I can recognize when the negativity bias has taken over the driving seat. You'll still feel it, but you'll understand it, so you'll be less likely to feel anxious about it. Again, it's all about adopting that helicopter view, through which everything begins to make sense.

While it is necessary from time to time to take stock of how we're doing, there's a more positive way for us to do this than getting competitive with or feeling less than our peers. When you catch yourself in a spiral of self-comparison, Leon Festinger wisely suggests interrupting this pattern with "temporal comparison"; a lesser-known theory but one that yields far more encouraging results. According to this theory, our best bet is to compare ourselves today with how we were in the past. We don't involve anybody else in the picture. By focusing on ourselves alone, it shifts our thinking from one-upmanship (anxiety-inducing) to positive self-improvement.

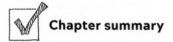 **Chapter summary**

- *Comparing yourself to others, particularly via social media, never has a positive outcome. In fact, it's fueling your anxiety.*

- *Though you might feel insecure or anxious or not good enough when looking at other people's social media, remember this: The fact that they are putting so much* of themselves out there, for likes and followers, might reflect their own feelings of insecurity, even if they appear confident on the surface. Give that some thought.

- Don't be hard on yourself. Everybody does it, it's a part of human nature; social media just makes it inescapable in the twenty-first century.

- Everything you see on social media is a compilation of other people's best bits; you're comparing your own "behind the scenes" with everyone else's "highlights reel."

- Your perception of others is skewed via social media. What you see is most certainly not what you get. What you get, you distort. Interestingly, while the negativity bias leads us to outweigh the negative in our own lives, social comparison theory suggests that we are simultaneously more likely to overestimate the presence of positivity in other people's lives. Go figure.

- Others' failures or successes are not a benchmark for your own worth.

- Instead of trying to be as good or better than everyone else, focus all your efforts on being the best version of yourself. Shift from social comparison to temporal comparison; it's healthier.

- Food doesn't taste better when it's been photographed for Instagram.

- You don't have to document your relationships on social media to justify them. In fact, the best things in life can happen off social media.

- *"If it's not on social media, it means it didn't happen," is a sentence that just shouldn't exist.*

- *JOMO (joy of missing out) is the new FOMO (fear of missing out), and I'm embracing it wholeheartedly.*

- *Nobody looks that good in the morning. #Filters.*

- *If you turn to social media for gratification or a confidence boost, ask yourself why.*

- *Even the people who seem to have the best lives on social media will have their own struggles, their own crosses to bear.*

- *There's no easier way to underestimate the prevalence of others' negative emotions than through social media, where they just don't show it.*

- *Try to have at least an hour or two a day when your phone and all access to social media is out of reach.*

- *Focus your attention instead on meaningful connections with the people in your life who matter.*

- *Spend more time doing things that make you forget to check your phone.*

- *Whether you put it on social media or not, feel comfortable in your own skin.*

Relationships can help and hinder your well-being

OUR RELATIONSHIPS HAVE a huge impact on both our experience of anxiety (in fact, they can sometimes contribute to our anxiety) and our eventual recovery from that horrible low point where it seems to govern our entire existence. For me, when I first fell apart, I cut myself off from my social circle, but in retrospect, I needn't have. I just didn't want to burden anyone with my troubles or drag anyone down with me, and I knew that I wasn't exactly fun to be around. I didn't want to leave my house, and I spent most of my time feeling upset.

Although shutting yourself away from the world is not the best way to handle anxiety, sometimes, if it's particularly bad, you just need a little break—a hall pass, a moment to bring yourself back to basics, rest, and rejuvenate. As it happens, it's in this time where your true friends will shine through. The keepers will be there regardless; they'll sit with you and distract you and allow you to feel the way you feel, and they will try their best to empathize. They will understand why you feel the need to take a step back, but they won't let you retreat to the point of no return. They will listen, and even if they've never felt a flutter of anxiety in their own lives, they will respect that, for you, it's a real struggle. We will all go through hard times, and a good relationship—be it a friendship, a family relationship or a romantic one—should be able to endure the bad times and not just be there for the highlights.

As you read this chapter, I want you to think long and hard about the relationships in your life. Are they serving you well? Are there any relationships that affect you negatively? Are these relationships worth having? Do they stress you out? Do they fuel your anxiety? We've all found ourselves embroiled in a toxic relationship at one point or another. It could be a boss, a peer, an ex-anyone. It might be a friend who expects too much of you or has their own ideas about what friendship means. It might be a friend you grew up with and, sure, you were the yin to his or her yang back then, but now it feels a little forced, and you know your core values and outlook on life no longer align. That's okay. Sometimes one of the most harmful things we can do to our sense of well-being is maintain relationships that cause us stress.

If you're really struggling right now and, like me, you need to take some of the pressure off (especially when it comes to maintaining your social life), my advice with your key relationships is this: just bare all so they can understand—or try to—what you're going through. Tell them how you're feeling, in person preferably, and that you're taking it upon yourself to find your own way through, that you need their support, but that when they don't hear from you or don't see you at a social gathering, it's in no way a reflection on them or how you feel about them; it's you needing to do what you need to do to find your feet again.

I felt an added weight of anxiety, on top of what I was already dealing with, in trying to keep up with social appointments. At the time, I had a friend who was getting married and organizing her bachelorette party. To everyone else, this was a chance to go wild, have fun and let loose, but as I was finding it difficult to even go around the corner for milk, the prospect of such an event overwhelmed me entirely. I knew (or at least I hoped) I wouldn't always feel this way and I wanted to be there for my friend, but I also knew that I needed to allow myself the freedom of opting in or out of whatever I felt I was able for. I had to do what was right for me. I didn't go, and she understood, and I lifted away some of the stress by giving myself the luxury of choice. The last thing you need is to feel as though you have to please everyone else. Tell the people who matter that you have to put yourself first for a while so that you can lighten the load on your shoulders. The good ones will understand.

Dr. Coyne says of relationships:

> Time spent with emotionally warm adults in whose company you feel safe and at ease can give you a wonderful feeling of well-being. One of the best ways to lower stress levels and relax your body is to spend time with really genuine and warm people, those you can cry with and those who you can laugh with, in essence those that you can be FULLY YOU with.
>
> Being with warm people is the ultimate mood changer and the answer is found in your brain. A meeting of minds or a good laugh with the right person can activate optimal levels of your "feel-good'" brain chemicals and drastically lower your stress levels, by relaxing your heart rate and blood pressure. The endorphins can act as a natural pain reliever, while the serotonin release can serve as an antidepressant or mood-lifter without the side effects.

As for those who don't get it, or are unwilling to try and get it, do you really want that person in your life?

It's time to prioritize the people who are worthy of your time and energy, the people who accept you just as you are, and the people who will be there for you whether you crave a night in in your PJs or you're ready to go sky-diving.

Not all of these people need to be exactly like you; I have plenty of friends who are very different from me, friends who I would look at and think, "Wow, they're just capable of anything and nothing scares them." They know I'm a bit sensitive and delicate, and I probably can't stomach as many shots as they can on a night out, but they don't think any less of me for it. In fact, they have a huge amount of respect for the fact that I just know myself and my body, what suits me and what doesn't, and that I make no apologies for it. I don't try to be someone I'm not. And if for one moment someone didn't accept that, well, they would no longer be a priority in my life. As you get older, you realize that life is too short for pandering to people who have a negative impact on your existence.

Career-wise (or maybe you're still in school or university) my advice is to find your ally. Even if it's just one person with whom you can share how you're feeling, this makes being at work, school or college all the more bearable if you're having an off day.

Back when I first started to feel like the clouds were closing in on me, I felt one hundred times worse because I tried to pretend that I was fine. Think about it; you're smiling on the outside but you're crumbling on the inside, and then your boss turns around, completely unaware of how you're feeling, only to ask you to do something that you think is impossible.

You crumble even further. I cannot stress enough just how much having to pretend that you're "fine" when you feel anything but can compound your feelings of anxiety.

For me, when I eventually went back to work, I decided to just be upfront about how I was feeling. I didn't broadcast it to everyone as they walked into the office, but I would tell colleagues who I'd become close to, as well as my direct boss, and it made my life so much easier. That way, if I was having a bad day, I didn't feel under any added pressure to be cartwheeling around the office. I was still able to get my work done and do it to a high standard, but it was a relief to know that it was okay that I was not okay. They were understanding.

Now I was particularly lucky. I went to work with a popular women's magazine (IMAGE) where we were encouraged to write regularly about things like mental health and stress management, so, for me, it was the perfect opportunity to say, "Oh, yeah I sometimes feel this way, too," and, sure enough, there were plenty of others who felt the same. I appreciate that this is not always the case in other working environments, but while it might not be the go-to topic of conversation among coworkers (or classmates) you can be sure other people are feeling it too or will have experienced it in the past. They will empathize.

Now I'm not saying that you should go for a job interview and say, "By the way, I have anxiety" (not that it should reflect negatively on you if you do). But just find your person—it could be a colleague, a friend or even your favorite teacher at school or a college professor who you think would be understanding (if, for example, you need more time on a project)—and confide in them. It requires bravery, yes, and it can feel risky, of course, but, for me, during times of intense anxiety, it made the world of difference, and not one person I confided in made me feel bad about it.

On a more macro level, talking about our mental health struggles in the same way we would talk about a sore muscle is important. Eventually, my hope is that we will get to a point where people are no longer afraid to say that they are struggling with anxiety. We will no longer perceive it as a sign of weakness, and, thus, we will feel the anxiety a whole lot less. I don't doubt it for one second.

I credit a lot of my sense of wellness today to the most important relationships in my life—my family and my partner, Barry. I wasn't in my relationship with him all that long when I started to struggle, and I presumed he'd run for the hills. It's not what he signed up for and it was anything but fun. It was a huge internal pressure; I felt guilty that he had to watch me fall apart and mope around all day. Lots of people would have walked, and you wouldn't blame them, but this guy—though scared as hell—stopped me every time I brought it up, and reminded me that he wasn't going anywhere. He didn't separate himself from me, just because he wasn't feeling the same as I was. He was also genuinely clueless about what to do, but he made an active decision to help me in any way he could, even if that was just being there for me and letting me cry about my latest panic attack. Instead of saying, "You'll be okay" or "You'll get through this," he would say, "We are going to find a way through this together," and that realization—that I wasn't in it alone—was a huge comfort.

Sometimes you just need to trust the people who love you, let them love you, let them be there for you, stop making apologies, and allow yourself to depend on them. It's okay; we all need help sometimes. And it is this help, from meaningful connections with others, that will see you through.

Then there was my darling mum, whom I wish I could just share with all of you, but I'm sure yours is just as good too. I vividly remember a string of days where she wouldn't leave my side. She was determined to find a way through (all of which I've mapped out in this book). She lay beside me in bed as I tried but failed to sleep. She would gently stroke my face in the same way she would have when I was a kid. She even tried to sing me to sleep one time, and we both wound up crying at the sentiment of her chosen song—"True Colors." She wanted nothing more than for me to not be afraid, and to know that I would be okay.

On another afternoon, when she found me sitting on the floor of the shower, yet again in tears, she bundled me up in towels, sat me down on the bed and, with a pen and paper, wrote down every possible thing we could try—and try we would—to reduce the physical symptoms of anxiety, alleviate the associated depression and help me feel like myself once more. Bit by bit, she put me back together again.

So, decide who in your life you can lean on, and don't be afraid to do just that; lean on them. These people will remind you that you're not alone, and they'll motivate you to do the necessary work to get to that point of owning your anxiety.

 Chapter summary

- *Even though you might feel like hiding under your covers, don't cut yourself off from people.*

- *We are social creatures; we experience all of the feel-good hormones when engaging with people (well, the ones who make us feel good).*

- *At the same time, you might want to take your foot off the gas; any good friend will understand your need for this right now.*

- *Be honest about the relationships that give you nothing but grief. Can you walk away from them?*

- *If you have to endure some relationships that aren't ideal, learn to distance yourself emotionally.*

- *Stop trying to change things if the people involved are consistently difficult. It's not on you.*

- *Don't be afraid to tell people that you're feeling a little overwhelmed. The more we hide our anxiety, the more we perpetuate the idea that it isn't normal or okay.*

- *You will feel so much better for having shared your thoughts and feelings with someone who is willing to listen.*

- *Rely on your family and friends. It's okay; we all need emotional support sometimes.*

CHAPTER
14

Shut up and breathe

IN THE MIDST of my worst days, one thing that was sure to grind my gears was being told to "breathe." "Just breeeeathe," they said. Really? Yeah, like I haven't tried that already.

I was frustrated as hell, as I am sure you are too. Breathing did sweet f*ck all as far as I was concerned, but every single thing I read and every professional I encountered—even the ones I had so much faith in—was adamant that this was a major missing piece in the puzzle of my recovery and ongoing management of anxiety.

Though mindfulness became a hot trend right around the time of my experience, I was skeptical that it was anything other than a waffly, spiritual philosophy for letting inconsequential everyday stress roll off your back. I could see how it might be beneficial to someone who had the tendency to overreact or someone who spent all day on tense business calls, but for me—someone who was struggling to even go out and socialize—I felt nothing more than a temporary slowing down of breath and no long-term ass-kicking benefits. I needed more.

But here's where I learned yet another lesson (which, I'll admit, took a really long time): I was too impatient to give it a chance to even see if it would yield any long-term benefits. Patience and mindfulness or meditation absolutely need to go hand in hand; otherwise, you wind up back at the first paragraph of this chapter. The thing is, at the same time, you can't go beating yourself up for being impatient either (which I did, relentlessly).

From my experience, meditation is simply a term used to describe the time spent paying attention to the present movement, usually involving really focused breathing.

Like it or not, there are now countless published studies that demonstrate the benefits of ongoing mindfulness and meditation, especially when it comes to stress and anxiety. At a certain point I decided I needed to get down off my high horse and consider that maybe, there was more to the act of breathing than the basic function of keeping us alive or the more extreme idea of having to adopt a monk-like existence.

Throughout the period of time in which I experienced anxiety on a more acute level, I would regularly meet with my therapist (a Cognitive Behavioral Therapist, to be specific, but more on this in Chapter 16). After a particularly bad episode, it usually went like this: "I was doing fine and then I just had a blip and wound up feeling really, really anxious again, back at square one, I don't know what I did wrong."

She'd nod, smile, and say that I'd done nothing wrong, but then asked, "Have you been practicing your mindfulness?" Cue inner monologue. "Ugh, please. It doesn't make a difference FFS!"

But I hadn't even tried, and she knew it (thankfully, she was more patient with me than I ever could have been with myself).

You see, I'd only ever sit down and force myself to meditate right in the middle of a bad day. But that kind of pressure is never going to work, hence I never felt any of the benefits. (Another note: The word "force" should never appear in the same sentence as "meditation," otherwise you've missed the point entirely.)

In terms of showing your anxiety who's boss, I cannot stress just how important it is to keep doing what works for you to maintain your optimal state of wellness when you're *already* feeling good, not just when you feel bad. This, I sucked at.

When I felt good, I let all of my efforts slide. I didn't want to acknowledge the fact that I had anxiety at all, I didn't want to remind myself of the bad times—and I especially didn't want to sit there for twenty minutes a day staring into space only to wind up berating myself for my complete inability to live in the moment. To be honest, I feared that spending time with my own thoughts would only bring the anxiety hurtling back, so I did everything I could to avoid that.

How I eventually got my head around it though was in the idea of repetition—practice makes perfect—and, more importantly, understanding how giving yourself a time-out to just breathe can impact your physiology. So, for me, it was less about the spiritual stuff like aligning the chakras and connecting to some higher power, and more about the science.

You see, it's never going to be one session that fixes everything, though you will feel at least more relaxed for a while afterward. It's only when you make it a habit and incorporating it into your daily routine that you'll notice the benefits. When you slow down your breathing for a period of time and focus on long, deep breaths, you reduce your body's production of cortisol, the stress hormone. If you keep doing this every day, you reduce your body's cortisol levels over time and keep them low on a long-term basis.

The more you give your body the chance to feel this relaxation, the more you give your body the chance to accept this feeling as its natural state, and the more you train your body to return to this natural state after something stressful occurs.

It might feel like being permanently on edge is your body's resting position right now, but the more you enable your body to experience this chill, which you have the power to do (exercise: sing along to Snap's "I've Got the Power" and enjoy a little *Bruce Almighty* moment), the more familiar your body becomes with it. I promise.

Despite what you might have read elsewhere, it's really not about what you think about or don't think about during this rest period, or about how you sit or where you are or what's around you. It is literally just about allowing yourself to feel physically relaxed, slowing down your heart rate and becoming entirely aware of that relaxed feeling, enjoying it, and doing it again and again. Simply put, right now you're on high alert and anxiety is your go-to state of being. By meditating regularly, your body gets more and more breaks from the anxiety and that can only be a good thing, but if you're still rolling your eyes, don't just take my word for it.

For a long time, there was little more than anecdotal evidence to show the ways in which meditation could change your brain, but in recent years a significant number of promising studies have come to the fore, converting many a skeptic.

While lots of studies based their conclusions on participants' feedback, e.g., telling the researchers that they felt "great" afterward (not exactly the thorough scientific proof we're looking for, is it?), the ones that caught my attention were those that looked at before-and-after brain scans, and the effects that meditation had on the production of cortisol (known to many an anxiety sufferer as public enemy number one).

One 2013 study in the journal *Health Psychology*[4] showed a direct link between mindful breathing and lowered cortisol, while another that focused on medical students, who deal with lots of stress, showed that participants' cortisol levels reduced from 381.93 nmol/L (SD 97.74) to 306.38 nmol/L (SD 90.95) over a four-day period—which according to science people, is all kinds of significant. As for the brain scans, a study published in *PLOS One*[5] a journal published by the Public Library of Science in the US, showed that after an eight-week course of mindfulness practice, the brain's amygdala appeared to shrink. As interpreted by *Scientific American*[6] when the amygdala shrinks, the prefrontal cortex—that's the part of our brain that's associated with awareness, concentration and decision making—becomes thicker, which is a good thing.

The "functional connectivity" between these regions—i.e., how often they are activated together—also changes. The connection between the amygdala and the rest of the brain gets weaker, while the connections between areas associated with attention and concentration get stronger. The scale of these changes correlates with the number of hours of meditation practice a person has done, says

Adrienne Taren, a researcher studying mindfulness at the University of Pittsburgh:

> **The picture we have is that mindfulness practice increases one's ability to recruit higher-order, prefrontal cortex regions in order to down-regulate lower-order brain activity. In other words, with meditation, our more primal responses to stress seem to be superseded by more thoughtful ones.**

Apart from stress, meditation has been proven to have a significant effect on our experience of pain, too. And that's when things all kind of clicked into place with me, perhaps because pain is more tangible than feelings of anxiety in the body and easier to put your finger on. Over the past few years, I have experienced a lot of lower back pain. Once, after straining my back while exercising, I proceeded, as we all instinctively do, to walk around holding myself up straight, tight and tensing my muscles in a bid to prevent further damage. But by holding myself in such a way, I was perpetuating the pain and not giving my muscles a chance to relax. For me, it was actually my thought processes that made me tighten up—"I have to be really careful or I'll hurt myself more"—rather than the presence of pain. My mind was trying to protect my body and, like always, it was trying a little too hard.

What made a difference was bringing my attention to my breathing. For example, bending down to tie my shoe-laces was something I considered very carefully, which made me tense up, which, in turn, made the movement near impossible. When I tried again, this time breathing deep into my belly and exhaling fully, I let my body relax physically, and just like that, I could fold over and reach my feet. Now the pain wasn't entirely gone—I'm not for a second saying it was all in my head and I could sim-ply breathe the pain away—but by consciously breathing through these kinds of basic movements that we don't think twice about, I helped to alter my body's physiology. The pain made for an inconvenient reminder to keep bringing my attention back to my breathing, and instead of bracing to protect myself, my back muscles loosened and went back to normal far sooner than they had ever done before. Within twenty-four hours I went from not being able to bend at all to moving around freely, and considering my physiotherapist hadn't as much as mas-saged my back or given me any pain relief or exercise to do, I had a newfound respect for just how powerful our breathing can be, vowing never to give this innate tool that we all share such a hard time in future.

And that's probably enough science for one chapter.

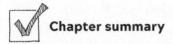 **Chapter summary**

- *Behold my essential tips for owning your meditation practice:*

- *If you're really up the wazoo, or you just love a good to-do list, mark time to meditate in your diary.*

- *Before you leap out of bed in the morning, breathe in and out four times, slowly.*

- *When inhaling, breathe deep down into your belly; you need to see your belly expand, not your shoulders rising (the latter kind of breathing is stress-inducing).*

- *Start small. Don't try to take on a twenty-minute meditation on day one, try something achievable like a one-minute sitting.*

- *Cut yourself some slack. Most people find this really difficult.*

- *Rely on apps, such as Calm, which really make it so much easier. You don't need to do anything other than follow their guided meditations as they tell you to breathe in and out.*

- *Don't get frustrated when thoughts pop into your head. They are going to come along whether you like it or not, and if you get angry about it, what's there to gain?*

- *In my honest opinion, it doesn't really matter what you're thinking about, in fact trying not to think is extremely anxiety-inducing for me.*

- *Think about whatever the hell you want as long as you retain some semblance of awareness (and nonjudgment!); as long as you're breathing nice and deep and slow, I don't think it matters.*

- *Counting really helps. I've tried so many variations but what works for me is this: breathe in for a count of four, breathe out for a count of eight, rest for a count of four.*

- *After a few rounds of count-breathing, just let your breathing fall back into a natural rhythm for a while.*

- *You don't need to sit cross-legged with your back super straight if this is not the kind of position you'd normally relax in. I prefer to lie down on my bed.*

- *Having said that, you don't need to be at home to take a few mindful moments. Sometimes, I decide to hone in on my breathing on the bus or while I'm working; it just feels nice. I even take boring ad breaks in the middle of my favorite TV shows as a chance to check in with my breathing. Just be sure to mute the TV.*

- *Don't expect any life-altering, existential, out-of-body experiences. (I did because I had read Eat Pray Love—it doesn't happen for most of us.)*

- *Stop thinking of "mindfulness" or "meditation" as some sort of art form or trend that you have to be skilled at, as this could put you under unnecessary pressure. Instead, think of it as nothing more than breathing slowly while taking your head out of your phone. You're already really good at breathing, otherwise you wouldn't be reading this.*

- *Some days, you'll just have too much going on in your head to get the benefit; this happens to me a lot and that's okay. Make a mental note to give it another shot when you've less urgent things running through your brain.*

- *Remember that it's called a practice because it's not something you nail on day one—it's something you're always working on. It's a skill that you develop over time, an, eventually, it becomes a very reliable tool in managing your anxiety.*

- *Do it as often as you like, but try for at least once a day.*

- *If you want to shake things up a little, try Ujjayi breathing (see page 157).*

- *I certainly found it harder to try to take a moment's peace if my room was cluttered. A peaceful environment helps, but you don't need the sound of bells and forty candles to do the job (though, if that works for you, by all means go ahead).*

- *Don't not meditate because you feel "fine." This is a mistake I kept making. Even if you don't feel you need it because you're not experiencing anxiety, enjoy it for all its many untold benefits, among which are better sleep, clarity, better concentration and better reactions to negative things.*

- *If you're skeptical like I was, focus only on the science. You just can't argue with the facts that show how this simple task can positively affect your physiology.*

Exercise
HOW TO MASTER UJJAYI BREATHING

When you've come to terms with the power of breathing, you can move on to Ujjayi breathing, which is rooted in yoga.

There are many different breathing techniques out there, some helpful, some just plain ridiculous. At the crux of them all, however, is a little bit of mental focus on the physical aspects of breathing, which takes your mind away from anxious thoughts. In a lot of cases, it's less so the fancy-pants breathing technique itself you can thank, and more so the general act of mindfulness where your brain is focused on the task at hand. In this regard, you could well argue that breathing in and out while patting your head and rubbing your stomach at the same time has much the same effect. It probably would, and at least you might have a giggle doing it, but the reason I like Ujjayi breathing in particular is not just for the way it distracts me; the physicality of your breath here has an instantly relaxing effect on your body. In fact, I like it so much that I spend as much time as I can breathing in this way, whether I'm on the bus, lying down watching TV, typing on my laptop—wherever. It's big in yogic circles but you don't actually have to practice yoga at all to enjoy the benefits of this technique. Now, let's get to it.

What exactly is Ujjayi breathing?
Well, it's nothing new. In fact it's ancient—a wave-like breathing technique, made popular among yogis, that is both relaxing and energizing at the same time. Translated as "victorious breath" and often referred to as "oceanic

breath," when done right, it should result in a long and very smooth breath—so nothing erratic or forceful—that you can audibly hear. Go to an intermediate or advanced yoga class and you will hear those more experienced exhaling with a soothing sound, similar to the rolling in and out of a wave on the shore.

How do you do it?

The first thing to note here is that Ujjayi breathing takes a little time to get right and, at first, you might feel like you're just sighing. Be patient with yourself.

Don't put in too much effort either, the point is to feel relaxed.

1. Ideally, sit or lie down, back elongated, legs crossed, if that feels good for you. It doesn't really matter where you are or how you're positioned, as long as you're comfortable.
2. Inhale gently through your nose, filling your stomach with air. I once read that the Ujjayi breathing is easiest to master when you imagine sipping your breath in through a straw; you're not gulping in the air. But don't open your mouth!
3. Hold the breath for a second or two, whatever feels comfortable.
4. Exhale gently by constricting the back of the throat. This creates the tiniest bit of constriction to the air leaving your body. The word "constriction" sounds counterproductive to meditation, I know, but if you control the release of air like this, allowing it to exhale evenly and smoothly—as opposed to forcefully and quickly—you feel noticeably more relaxed (even if you don't feel relaxed mentally).

5. As you exhale, slowly, you should be naturally making a soft whooshing, wave-like sound. It's similar in a way to the sound you would make when trying to fog up a mirror (except this time your mouth is closed). This happens because of the throat constriction, so you shouldn't have to force out a sound. It should come from your throat like a whisper. It shouldn't be raspy or grating, it should be quite pleasant to hear, as though you're listening to yourself sleeping.
6. Repeat.
7. When you have this down, try to nail this breathing technique in lots of different scenarios, standing up, walking, doing some stretches.
8. If you struggle to get the sound right, start by whispering *HAAAA* with your mouth open.

Why is it good?
- It increases the amount of oxygen in your blood.
- It relieves tension and relaxes nerves instantly.
- It helps you to harness energy.
- It has a huge balancing effect on your entire cardio-respiratory system.
- It relieves feelings of frustration or anger.
- It improves your concentration when you need to focus.
- It generates internal body heat, and as your core becomes warm on the inside it's like a massage for your lungs.
- It is also said to reduce pain, and strengthen the nervous and digestive systems.

How to sleep like a baby

OF ALL THE side effects that my anxiety brought to the fore, sleeplessness and the imbalance of cortisol and melatonin were definitely among the worst and the hardest to correct.

Sleep problems are among the most common issues facing those with anxiety. Though cortisol is primarily the stress hormone, each morning we all release a certain amount of it to get us going for the day ahead. Its function here is not to stress you out or make you feel fearful as you rise—your biology isn't *quite* that cruel—but without this little boost, we'd remain in a constant state of lethargy.

Where it becomes a problem, however, is when you're already experiencing a prolonged state of stress and anxiety. At this point, you've got enough cortisol in your body to wake up a whole village, let alone yourself, and so you really don't need any extra help in that regard. What is meant as a slight boost of invigoration to someone who's anxiety-free winds up feeling like a tsunami of unforeseen fear to you or me. If you've noticed and wondered why your anxiety feels significantly worse first thing in the morning, this is precisely the reason.

For me, because my cortisol was just at a constant high, as a side effect, I pretty much stopped producing melatonin altogether. Melatonin is the wind-down hormone, and its job is to prepare us for sleep. Imagine it like two waves on a graph, both of which are always in rhythm and codependent on each other's balance. We begin in the morning with a spike of cortisol, then, after a few hours, this begins to slowly decrease and, eventually, the cortisol should have left our bodies, at which point, the melatonin, which took a back seat during the day so you could live your life without drifting off, begins its necessary ascent. At its corresponding peak, we go to bed and fall asleep. Or so we should.

Melatonin is one of my favorite hormones, probably because I was starved of it for so long. In fact, I really didn't get a full night's sleep for about three or four months straight. At first I didn't exactly feel tired, I just lay there staring at the ceiling, totally wired—after a short time, it was not a pretty picture. I soon understood why sleep deprivation is used as a form of torture. I might have had an hour or two at about 5 AM, but it was anything but restorative; I was plagued with cortisol. Then, without the need for any kind of alarm, my anxiety would reef me from my brief hiatus (although even in my dreams I was anxious, too, so I just couldn't catch a break).

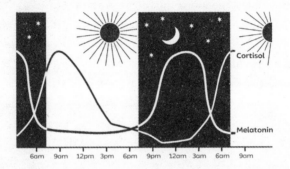

In fact, it wasn't a flurry of anxious thoughts that first woke me, it was always the physical feeling of cortisol building up in my limbs. Every morning, it was as though my body had produced enough stress hormone to take on a cheetah, but, with no cheetah in front of me, all of the excess hormone just reverberated around my body, eventually settling into what felt like crystallized anxiety. I could almost touch it.

It was in my back, it was in my shoulders, my legs and my arms, it was even in my gums. It was horrible. It was like waking up every morning on the worst day of the flu. I'd thrash around the bed, not quite fully conscious yet, trying to work these hormones out of my body. Then, fully awake, along would come the tears and the Jesus-I'm-really-not-in-a-good–way-am-I? realization.

As you can imagine, when you don't really understand what's happening to you or why, having such a physical reaction can be really scary, and thus you begin to fear the physical symptoms of anxiety more than the thoughts that come with them. I would dread going to bed, because: (a) I'd never get a proper sleep; and (b) I was so fearful of waking up in the morning and having to go through the cortisol hit.

During my five-horrible-days-in-a-row spells and other intense occasions, my boyfriend brought me back to my parents' house in the hope that sleeping in my old bed might be a welcome comfort. It wasn't—nothing helped—and each morning there, my mother would have to pour me a bath with Epsom salts so that my muscles could start to soften. Eventually, they would, but my emotions would be left in the gutter, reeling from the experience. Then she'd go to work, and I'd ring her at regular intervals, in tears asking what I was going to do and why I had to feel this way.

This was my existence and my pattern for what felt like far too long. I was awake, fearful, I went to bed, fearful, I woke up even more fearful and I cried several times a day. So, when it came to addressing the physical side of my anxiety, this lack of sleep and excess cortisol was at the top of my priority list. All I wanted was a good night's sleep and to wake up feeling rested and ache-free. Not too much to ask, I think.

While my experience was certainly on the more extreme end of the spectrum, lots of things can interrupt this careful balance of hormones in our bodies. An obvious one is staring at bright screens late at night or getting yourself jacked up on caffeine in the latter half of the day. Stress and anxiety are, obviously, natural enemies of sleep because to sleep soundly, we need to turn down the lights on our worries. But here's the thing: While anxiety will affect your sleep, a lack of sleep will also, in turn, increase your anxiety. So you have to intervene and proactively break the cycle. It's been suggested by various studies that by relieving our sleeping troubles we can and should be able to alleviate mental health symptoms, such as anxiety.

According to *Harvard Health*[7] a normal sleeper cycles between two major categories of sleep every ninety minutes, although the length of time spent in one or the other changes as sleep progresses. The two sleep categories are: deep, quiet sleep; and REM (which you've probably heard of—no, not the band).

> During "quiet" sleep, a person progresses through four stages of increasingly deep sleep. Body temperature drops, muscles relax, and heart rate

and breathing slow. The deepest stage of quiet sleep produces physiological changes that help boost immune system functioning. Essential. The other sleep category, REM (rapid eye movement) sleep, is the period when people dream. Body temperature, blood pressure, heart rate, and breathing increase to levels measured when people are awake. Studies report that REM sleep enhances learning and memory and contributes to emotional health.

Although scientists are still trying to tease apart all the mechanisms, they've discovered that sleep disruption—which affects levels of neurotransmitters and stress hormones, among other things—wreaks havoc in the brain, impairing thinking and emotional regulation. In this way, insomnia may amplify the effects of anxiety (among other psychiatric disorders), and vice versa.

Even if you're not having a particularly hard time sleeping right now, it's very important that you have an understanding of and an appreciation for your sleep, and an awareness of how vital it is to your overall well-being.

Something I've never understood is how a lack of sleep, especially in professional circles, is often something that's bragged about, as though it's a badge of honor or something to be proud of. "I'm so busy, I average four hours a night, but that's what coffee was invented for, right?" Where not so long ago I might have said,

"Wow, fair play," I now think, "Hmm, that's not going to end well." In no way does being awake for twenty hours a day and sitting at a desk for that entire time equate with long-term success. You might make millions, but you'll be left emotionally bankrupt.

At this point, make a mental note to read *Thrive* by Arianna Huffington (of *Huffington Post* fame), in which she credits much of her success to the wonder of sleep—if you don't take my word for it, you'll certainly take hers.

When it came to restoring my own sleep pattern and finally giving myself the break I so needed, I made a decision to steer well clear of sleeping pills. I'm sure, on rare occasions, they're not the worst thing in the world, but I was concerned that they'd be too strong, knocking me out in the short term, but lacking in any real long-term benefits when it came to the very important task of reinstating my sleep equilibrium. I was also conscious of how certain sleeping pills can leave you on quite the downer the following day, and given how poorly I was already feeling, I certainly didn't want to go adding to that. Even if I didn't endure a comedown of sorts, I was also afraid that I'd wind up relying on them. With sleep, you really have to think about your overall well-being, and you have to think about getting it right for the long term, not just for one night.

As I was severely sleep deprived, my doctor—Dr. Fionnula McHale, who I'll refer to several times in forthcoming chapters—prescribed me with a course of melatonin, which is a tablet form of the hormone my body was supposed to be producing. In certain countries, you need a prescription for it; in others, you can simply get it over the counter. I cannot begin to tell you how hugely helpful this was over the long term, when taken on an initial short-term basis. Despite it being a natural supplement, however, I was still wary of becoming overly dependent on it. However, it kick-started my melatonin production so that I resumed my natural rhythm and, after a few weeks, I no longer needed it. Like any other supplement, you have to be careful about taking melatonin tablets when you're already producing the necessary amount for the ideal sleep, otherwise you could still wind up upsetting your sleeping pattern. If you think something like this would help you, you have to talk to a doctor first.

But I didn't stop there. After experiencing the ways in which a lack of sleep can damage your well-being, I became an expert sleeper; I had so much respect for sleep. In fact, to this day, when people brag about only getting in at 7 AM because they'd had such a crazy night out, I feel quietly smug in the knowledge that I, instead, slept like a bear.

I studied the subject relentlessly, intrigued to inform myself on all possible natural, side-effect-free ways to guarantee a good night's sleep. Prioritizing sleep was just one aspect of my recovery and management of anxiety, but, boy, was it a biggie.

How to restore your sleep

There are several things we can do on a day-to-day basis that help us to get our sleeping patterns back on track.

- Limit yourself to one cup of coffee per day (if at all) and make sure you're not taking in any caffeine after 3 PM. Caffeine increases cortisol.

- Limit your sugar intake. Sugar is a huge stimulant that affects the quality of your sleep. Sugar increases cortisol, and, as we know, too much cortisol equals poor sleep.

- Watch your alcohol consumption and, if you're a smoker, beware of that, too. Alcohol might help you fall asleep in the short term, but as its effects wear off, it causes you to wake up. And the sleep you do get is not good sleep. Nicotine is a stimulant that speeds up your heart rate and increases your thinking. If going cold turkey isn't an option, at least avoid both before bedtime.

- Go to bed *before* you're tired and, though it sounds like Captain Obvious has joined us once again, read a physical book—not a device.

- Cut yourself off from all technology at least two hours before you go to bed. Harsh light from phones, tablets, laptops and TVs stimulate the brain in such a way that's not conducive to sleep.

- Make sure you're going to bed in a clean room—all that Feng Shui sh*t actually makes a difference. A cluttered, disorganized room will leave your mind feeling much the same. Just ask Marie.

- "Sleep hygiene" is a term that doesn't just refer to having nice clean sheets, it's about maintaining a schedule and using your bedroom only for sleeping (or sex). Resist the urge to work on your laptop from under the duvet.

- Make sure you're getting exercise each day. Regular aerobic activity helps people fall asleep faster, and, what's more, you spend longer in that "deep sleep" stage.

- Use relaxation techniques. You can employ these at any time of the day to help wind down any feelings of anxiety, but they are particularly helpful before bed. If I'm feeling wired, I'll do a twenty-minute session with my Calm app—one that's specifically tailored for inducing sleep—and I'll usually drift right off before it's done.

- The 4-7-8 Sleeping Trick is hugely popular in the online wellness sphere (I first came across it via Harvard doctor Andrew Weil[8]) and is touted by sleep enthusiasts the world over as a technique that promises to have you fast asleep in sixty seconds. For me, it took a little longer, but it made me feel considerably sleepier within minutes, making it easier to eventually drift off, so it's certainly worth a try.

- According to Dr. Weil, you simply breathe in for four, hold for seven, and breathe out for eight, while making a slight whooshing noise. Repeat three times. The combination of 4-7-8, he claims, works as a natural tranquillizer, enabling more oxygen to permeate your lungs and brain, which reduces your body's stress levels, setting you up for a restful night's slumber.

  Dr. Weil says: "Once you develop this breathing technique by practicing it every day, twice a day, it will be a very useful tool that you will always have with you. Use it whenever anything upsetting happens—before you react. Use it whenever you are aware of internal tension. Use it to help you fall asleep. Use it to deal with food cravings. Great for mild to moderate anxiety, this exercise cannot be recommended too highly. Everyone can benefit from it."

- On top of these lifestyle changes, there are several natural remedies available to you. However, before you go down this route, be sure to consult with your doctor or a healthcare professional.

- Talk to your doctor or an herbalist about magnesium supplements, which you can take before bed; it helps your muscles to relax and it decreases cortisol. In fact, this mineral is responsible for over three hundred biochemical reactions in the body.

- If you've been taking magnesium for a while, and you've not been noticing the benefits, that's because magnesium is, according to experts, best taken alongside vitamin D, and vice versa, as both are necessary for each other's nutrient absorption. American sleep specialist Doc Parsley has recently come up with his own "sleep cocktail," combining magnesium with vitamin D3 (along with a small dose of melatonin and L-tryptophan). The effects of this combination are believed to not only make you fall asleep but improve the quality of your sleep. Again, consult your doctor before starting a supplement routine.

- Also popular in this regard are valerian root, herbal teas (such as lavender or chamomile), and anything that contains amino acid L-theanine like matcha.

- Try This Works Sleep Pillow Spray—I know it might sound like a gimmick, but as the name suggests it actually works. The manufacturers undertook extensive research to back up their claims. I'm a big fan.

- Get your hands on some concentrated Montmorency cherry juice—I love the brand Drink Cherry Active, but you can also find it in other juices and supplements. A 2010 study[9] demonstrated its natural effects and it's an easily available product that one of my go-to nutritionists, Kaman Ryan, speaks very highly of: "The tart Montmorency cherries are one of the best natural sources of melatonin and a 30 ml serving before bed is believed to help induce a restful night's sleep."

Chapter summary

- *A lack of sleep will fuel anxiety—it can even bring it on in the first place—so remember that as a factor if you're wondering why you feel anxious.*

- *Anxiety will impact on your sleep; it's a vicious cycle.*

- *Stressing about trying to sleep will only make things worse.*

- *Do everything you can to give yourself the best chance of a good night's sleep but don't worry if you just can't drift off. If you ever needed an excuse for a daytime nap, here it is.*

- *Understand what's going on hormonally with melatonin, and how it interplays with cortisol.*

- *Make the necessary lifestyle changes mapped out in this chapter.*

- *Talk to your doctor or a specialist about the options available to you, from magnesium to melatonin and everything in between.*

Why Cognitive Behavioral Therapy is everything

LIKE SLEEP, Cognitive Behavioral Therapy (CBT) deserves the word count of several theses. Alas, I only have space to give you a taste of why it worked for me.

It feels odd to introduce CBT as a standalone chapter, since much of what we've covered so far falls naturally under the umbrella of CBT. But that's how significant I believe it was for my recovery—and yours—and my long-term management of anxiety.

You might not have been explicitly aware of its presence in the book thus far. Basically, we are using CBT any time we observe our thought patterns, feelings, and behaviors, and seek to reinforce more helpful and positive alternatives.

Developed by Dr. Aaron Beck (of the Beck Institute, a leading international source for training, therapy and resources in CBT[10]) in the 1960s, it offers a set of invaluable life skills that you'll return to again and again. Today, I'm experienced enough to practice my CBT skills alone, but when I was right in the thick of it, attending one-on-one CBT sessions was yet another major piece of the puzzle that put me back together again. With CBT, you'll finally own it.

Going back to the beginning of my journey, one of the first things I knew I needed was the help of a professional, onto whom I could unload all of the conflict swirling around my head, without the worry of bringing them down with me.

That was easier than dumping my suffering onto someone who was emotionally involved with me, because then I'd have the added worry that they were worrying about me, and suddenly we're all worrying unnecessarily. A professional is trained in the art of separating themselves from the emotion of the client in front of them.

I spent months in regular counseling—or traditional talk therapy, as I like to refer to it—addressing my anxiety and how awful I was feeling, dredging up a lot of what had happened in the past. While this was certainly helpful in terms of figuring out why I was feeling the way I was, looking back, I was intuitive enough to figure this part out on my own. At a certain point, I was just done talking about it. In each session, I'd indulge in my suffering to such an extent that I'd leave the therapist's office feeling no better. Don't get me wrong, this type of therapy can certainly be cathartic, and it's essential that you are prepared to get this up close and personal with your own experience—if you're the kind of person who's just less in tune with themselves. But I needed practical intervention. I needed clarity. I needed diagrams. I needed to focus less on the past and more about how to improve my right here, right now, and my future. I needed a list of dos and don'ts. When I had established that, yes, I *was* suffering with anxiety and that, yes, this is probably *why*, I'd achieved all that I could with talking therapy. That's when I changed tactics and shifted toward CBT. This was a game-changer, and one that gave me the many what-am-I-going-to-do-about-it? answers I so needed, all of which I've mapped out in this book for you to employ in your own way.

For those who've heard the term but aren't quite sure of what's involved, CBT is a form of talk therapy in which you work with your therapist to identify and change the way you think (cognitive) and the way you act (behavioral), using a mixture of proven techniques. It's based upon the idea—or, rather, the fact—that our thoughts, feelings, and behaviors are all intrinsically linked. Our thoughts influence our feelings and our feelings influence our behaviors that, in turn, can influence our thoughts. It's a very simple theory that's been proven to be particularly successful in the treatment of both anxiety and depression.

I became an instant fan because it focuses entirely on the now (rather than the past, which you can't do a whole lot about today), and approaches mental health from a more scientific perspective, looking at our cognitive model and how we can rewire our thinking so that it no longer affects our feelings and behaviors negatively.

At the center of CBT, according to the Beck Institute, is the belief that—and you'll recognize this from Chapter 10—the way we perceive a situation is more closely connected to our reaction to it than the situation itself. For example, one person might be reading this thinking, "Wow! This sounds good, it's just what I've always been looking for!" so they feel positive and encouraged. Another person, however, might think to themselves, "Well, this sounds good, but I don't think I can do it." Their belief that they can't do it is inhibiting their chances of overcoming their anxiety. So, as clearly explained by the folks at Beck, it is not necessarily a situation that directly affects how people feel emotionally, but rather, how they think in that situation:

> When people are in distress, their perspective
> is often inaccurate and their thoughts may be
> unrealistic. Cognitive Behavioral Therapy helps
> people identify their distressing thoughts and

evaluate how realistic those thoughts are. Then they learn to change their distorted thinking. When they think more realistically, they feel better. The emphasis is also consistently on solving problems and initiating behavioral changes.[11]

A clearer picture of the connection between our cognition and our behavior might be this:

- Thoughts: I can't cope, I feel anxious so I must be anxious, something awful might happen.

- This influences our feelings: I feel anxious, fearful, overwhelmed, nervous, panicked.

- Then these feelings influence our behavior: I avoid situations, remain under the covers, opt out, stay safe, leave, go home, escape.

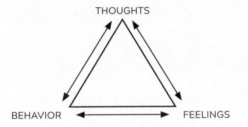

CBT helps to interrupt this self-perpetuating cycle.

While CBT comprises a variety of key tools and techniques, it also borrows from several other psychotherapeutic approaches—many of which you're already becoming familiar with in this book, such as positive psychology, acceptance therapy and mindfulness.

Every CBT therapist will employ different strategies upon talking to you about what it is that you're specifically dealing with, and that's another reason why I like it; there's no one-size-fits-all—so while I might be guilty of thinking negatively in one way, you might be fine with that but struggle with something else. What is common to all CBT therapists, however, is that you will be asked lots of questions to help you identify exactly your thought patterns and see where such thinking is unhelpful. As explained by Beck:

> The basic question to ask when a patient is reporting a distressing situation, emotion or dysfunctional behavior is: "What is going through your mind right now?" Once a therapist helps patients to identify their dysfunctional thinking, they help them gain more adaptive and accurate perspectives, especially by helping them examine the validity and usefulness of their thoughts. And once you identify one or all parts of this vicious cycle, you can change it. The therapist will also work with you on behavioral experiments to test the accuracy of their predictions and help you see things more clearly.[12]

I loved this idea of being given mental exercises, even some reading as homework. Again, I found it helpful, productive, and positive, as I was no longer just drowning in my own misery. I was owning my actions.

So if you're really struggling at the moment, sign yourself up for some one-on-one, or even group CBT sessions. Soon, you'll be so much better equipped to identify when your thinking has gone off on one, and thus be able to bring yourself back to center.

For me, some of the best exercises—and there are several, some of which you'll love, some of which you might not, so I won't list all of them here—are clearly mapped out on this genuinely brilliant (and free!) step-by-step CBT guide from GetSelfHelp.co.uk, which offers some of the best worksheets I've ever used. Now, it might feel like you're back in pre-school at first, but if you're feeling like this is too basic a task, ask yourself this: if we were all so good at identifying our thought patterns, feelings and behaviors, why would so many of us suffer so acutely with anxiety?

With any exercise or therapy, you will begin by choosing a situation that brought about feelings of anxiety. You'll identify your thoughts (what was going through your head at the time?), your feelings (how did you physically feel at the time?) and your behaviors (what did you do?). The ability to clearly and calmly name these elements will provide the foundation upon which you will build, with exercises such as The Helicopter View, The Fact or Opinion Approach, and your awareness of common mind traps which we covered earlier (see page 82).

When starting out, Dr. Coyne says:

> Using self-help worksheets is a good starting point to ascertain if CBT resonates with you, but delving deeper into your core beliefs about yourself, others and the world is best done in the safe hands of a qualified therapist.

Up next, we'll focus on a few key CBT exercises.

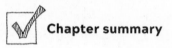 **Chapter summary**

- *For me, CBT, with practical exercises and techniques, was far superior to traditional talking therapy where I would just talk about how crap I was feeling.*

- *As our experience of anxiety is so wrapped up in our thoughts, feelings and behaviors, CBT is one of the most crucial steps you can take on the road to owning it.*

- *Get active with worksheets.*

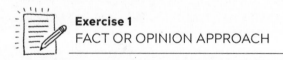 **Exercise 1**
FACT OR OPINION APPROACH

The Fact or Opinion Approach is one of the many helpful CBT skills at your disposal. This one is particularly favored by reputable psychiatric nurse Carol Vivyan on her website. Vivyan explains:

> At stressful times, we tend to be driven by our emotions and opinions, rather than fact, which create a vicious cycle by fueling each other. Our emotions strengthen our opinions, which in turn, intensify our emotions.

Hence, when we are stressed out or anxious, we believe the worst to be true, which makes us feel—you guessed it—even more stressed and anxious. This requires regular intervention.

What you need here is the ability to distinguish your opinions (which you can define as your own personal opinion, something that could be argued, something that's really fueled by emotion and something that's driven by your heart) from the facts (which are driven instead by the head, supported by rational thinking, evidence, and not at all up for dispute).

Instead of letting your emotions rule the roost, which they'd like to, facts are what you need to focus on here in order to make helpful changes and encourage more rational and calm thinking. This, in turn, will have a calming physiological effect on your acutely anxious body. But be patient with this one; it takes considerable time to stop yourself from jumping to the worst possible conclusion—I should know, I'm really bloody good at it.

So, what if, to begin with, you were to accept that many of your thoughts are opinion rather than fact? Would that make you less likely to be distressed by them? For example, I might have said to myself, "I cannot go on this group trip to Ibiza. I'm going to have a panic attack out of my comfort zone and it's going to be horrific and then I'll be so upset and never want to travel again." While I might not have been able to stop my mind from believing that the worst almost definitely would happen, I could at least step back and say, "Okay, your anxiety doesn't have a crystal ball into the future so you cannot know for sure that you're going to basically die on this trip; these are your anxiety-fueled assumptions talking, you might not feel this way if you weren't feeling anxious to begin with."

If you are able to label your thoughts as opinion, you will be less distressed by them, and you'll be able to accept that they are not necessarily a reality. This will make you better able to make wise and calm decisions about what to do next. I might still be filled with dread about all that could go wrong on a trip to Ibiza, but maybe, despite all of my opinions, I'd survive it and, better yet, have fun.

The key here, as always, is identification and acceptance. Your aim is not to undergo an instant personality transplant, suddenly feeling as cool as a cucumber about something that really rattles you, but to accept that these are just your anxious opinions and not facts. Here's Dr. Coyne's exercise recommendation:

> Next time you have a worrying thought, ask yourself whether your thought is a FACT or an OPINION.
>
> If it's an opinion, then I encourage you to look at the facts. What do you actually know about the situation?
>
> If it's a fact, then it is based on evidence and you are safer in making a choice about the best thing to do.

What did I know about going on a trip to Ibiza?

Well, if I momentarily tell my anxiety to take a hike, I know that my friends and my boyfriend will be there with me, so I'm not alone on a desert island. I know that nobody has a gun to my head, demanding that I must do this and that—when I'm there, I can do what I want, when I want. I know that I'll probably feel okay when I get there because, for me, the anticipation of something is always when I suffer the most. I had enough experience to know that this was often the case. I also know that I've had a panic attack before and I didn't die then, so I probably won't now. And if I'm to really push it, I also know that each panic attack simply gives me more experience in dealing with anxiety and more opportunities to put all of these exercises into action. Are we staying in the villa of a serial killer who has my name on his list of pending victims? Probably not.

For another example, say you are feeling tired, stressed, and anxious before an exam and you think, "I am so screwed, I am going to fail this exam."

Okay, is this a **fact** or an **opinion**?

Again, it's the latter. There is no evidence to suggest that you will absolutely fail your exam. This is not to say that your thought should not be acknowledged—I know, it makes you feel like sh*t, but it's important that you become aware that your negative thought about the exam could change if you were less anxious about it, or when you do it and *don't* fail, you'll wish you hadn't given yourself so much grief in the first place.

As we covered in Chapter 11, it's helpful to ask yourself "What would I think if I had no anxiety at all?" This will help you to determine whether something is based on cold, hard facts or anxious thoughts and opinions.

Exercise 2
BEHAVIORAL EXPERIMENT

This exercise is from PsychologyTools.com, a fantastic CBT online resource.

Cognitive Behavioral Therapy is very focused on behavioral experiments—I find these particularly helpful. They are practical and powerful information-gathering exercises that can be used to test the validity of what you're thinking or what you're certain is an absolute, unwavering fact (e.g., a belief that you are a weak person, which fuels your anxiety). They can also be used to gather evidence that confirms and supports new, more positive beliefs (e.g., you're not weak, you're sensitive). Essentially, when a belief is clearly specified—e.g., "I'm not good enough"—the evidence supporting it can be explored theoretically. By carrying out a simple thought-experiment, of which you'll find several throughout this book, new information may serve to confirm or disprove beliefs. It can really be quite the eye-opener. The aim with most behavioral experiments is to disrupt these negative beliefs and thought patterns, and replace them with more supportive alternatives, thus creating a positive impact on how you feel and on your behaviors.

The following CBT worksheet guides you through the essential steps required to plan and evaluate behavioral experiments. It lends itself nicely to planned experiments

("If I do X, then Y will happen") but can equally be used for data gathering ("If I ask X, then I will learn Y").

PREDICTION
What is your prediction?
What do you expect will happen?
How would you know if it came true?

EXPERIMENT
What experiment could test this prediction? (specifically name where & when)
What safety behaviors will need to be dropped?
How would you know your prediction had come true?

OUTCOME
What happened?
Was your prediction accurate?

LEARNING
What did you learn?
How likely is it that your predictions will happen in the future?

 Exercise 3
DETERMINING YOUR CORE VALUES

Find examples from both your career and personal life to ensure balance in your answers.

Step 1: Identify the times when you were HAPPIEST
- What were you doing?
- Were you with other people? Who?
- What other factors contributed to your happiness?

Step 2: Identify the times when you felt most PROUD
- Why were you proud?
- Did other people share your pride? Who?
- What other factors contributed to your feelings of pride?

Step 3: Identify the times when you were most FULFILLED
- What need or desire was fulfilled?
- How and why did the experience give your life meaning?
- What other factors contributed to your feelings of fulfillment?

Step 4: DETERMINE YOUR TOP VALUES based on your experiences of happiness, pride and fulfilment
- Why is each experience truly important and memorable?

Use the following list of common personal values to help you get started, and aim to choose about ten top values.

Adventure	Achievement	Authenticity
Balance	Autonomy	Authority
Compassion	Boldness	Beauty
Community	Citizenship	Challenge
Creativity	Contribution	Competency
Fairness	Determination	Curiosity

Friendships	Fame	Faith
Happiness	Growth	Fun
Honesty	Humor	Influence
Inner harmony	Justice	Kindness
Knowledge	Optimism	Learning
Love	Leadership	Meaningful work
Openness	Loyalty	Peace
Pleasure	Poise	Popularity
Recognition	Religion	Reputation
Respect	Responsibility	Security
Self-respect	Service	Spirituality
Stability	Success	Status
Trustworthiness	Wealth	Wisdom

Step 5: PRIORITIZE your top values

This is probably the most important step yet it's the most difficult, because you'll have to look deep inside yourself.

Write down your top values, in no particular order. Look at the first two values and ask yourself, "If I could satisfy only one of these, which would I choose?"

Keep working through your list, comparing each value with each other value, until your list is in the correct order.

Step 6: REAFFIRM your values

Check your top-priority values, making sure they fit with your life and your vision for yourself.

- Do these values make you feel good about yourself?
- Are you proud of your top three values?

CHAPTER
17

What you eat matters

THE SAYING "healthy body, healthy mind" rings true for me. When your body is well nourished and functioning optimally, your mind will always follow. In this chapter, we will look at the role of the diet in managing anxiety and a general guide to what to avoid or increase.

It's essential to mention at the outset that I cannot include a specific one-size-fits-all nutrition plan, with a daily meal guide or a list of supplements for you to rush out and stock up on, in the hope that, a few days later, you'll feel amazing. This would be doing you a disservice, and I urge you to resist the temptation to panic-buy every supplement that you've heard helps anxiety. This kind of generalized advice is seen too often in other books and advice columns and it can cause more problems in the long run.

Sure, a supplement may work wonders for 30 percent of anxiety sufferers, but there may be a percentage for whom it makes things worse. If we take supplements for things we do not need, their effect can be counterproductive.

We are all so different in our biological makeup as well as in how our bodies perform, hence personalized testing—or even just a one-to-one professional review—is so crucial. Beyond the common-sense basics of not over-doing stimulants such as caffeine and sugar, nutritional therapists (particularly if you go down the more holistic "functional medicine" route, which I advise) will look at each patient individually, taking into account several personal variants, for which you would undergo extensive testing, so that you will have the clearest diagnosis and a nutrition plan tailored to you. This is your best foot forward in terms of diet.

The truth about diet is this: You can work out seven days a week, eat like crap, and still have what appears to be a banging body, worthy of all those meaningless Instagram followers. Unfortunately, this does not mean that you are healthy *on the inside*—and that's precisely where it counts when we're talking about mental health (and all health, to be fair).

Only when my anxiety was really quite bad did I start to listen to the professionals—namely Dr. McHale—who told me that what I was eating really did matter. Now, I was hardly eating takeout five nights a week, but, because

I was an emotional wreck, the temptation to dive on a bag of Peanut M&Ms was near impossible to resist. I wanted comfort, and it usually came coated in sugar.

In my head, I'd rationalize it like this: "I feel sh*t, these might temporarily make me feel better, and I certainly don't care about having a flat stomach right now, when I feel like I'm falling apart." Sweet snacks certainly *do* give you a lift, because they taste good, but when it comes to anxiety, they do you no long-term favors and they actually make it all worse.

You have to take your diet seriously for this reason alone, otherwise all of your other efforts are pointless. For example, I could be doing all the yoga and mindfulness in the world, but if I'm chugging five sugary cups of coffee per day, stimulating my nervous system all the time, the yoga is hardly going to be worth my while. I may as well just sign up for a free course of panic attacks. Like it or not, this is yet another unavoidable and key component in your overall wellness—and the one that I certainly found the hardest to get on board with, so I understand if, at the end of this chapter, you feel like flinging this book against a wall.

At first, I was told that I should increase my dark green vegetable intake a lot, giving my brain the nutrients it needed to perform optimally and handle irrational thoughts, stresses and other stimuli. But I just wouldn't believe it. "There's no way this plate of kale is going to make me *not* have a panic attack; that's bullsh*t." Well, it won't, not in one day, but, over time, being mindful of what you put in your body absolutely *will* impact on your anxiety levels—and all of those key players, such as cortisol—in just the same way that your efforts elsewhere will add up over time.

So consider your "diet"—what you eat and drink—as entirely separate from the aesthetics of how you look, which isn't important as far as this book's concerned. As with everything else we've mapped out thus far, if we focus on short-term gains, we get nowhere. Unfortunately, to yield the benefits you want requires time, consistency, and patience.

To help you better understand the role of your diet in dealing with anxiety, I asked Dr. McHale to come on board.

She specializes in functional medicine, which seeks to look at the whole picture of a patient—lifestyle, diet, genetics, everything—rather than honing in on one particular symptom. In short, she looks beyond the point of seeing wellness as merely "the absence of disease." Instead, for her and others in her field, wellness is about vitality—feeling and functioning at your most optimal level on an ongoing basis.

Initially, I went to Dr. McHale complaining about my stomachaches, and talking to her gave me my first wake-up call and made me realize that, perhaps, there was more at play here than my digestive system. In fact, as we now know (far too much about my intestines), my digestive system wasn't to blame at all. When we both realized that it was stress and anxiety that was causing me so much physical upset, it was time to look at the natural ways in which I could better support my body so that it could handle stress in a healthier way—not *eliminate* stress but take it away from the super-high-alert, alarm-bells-ringing state of caution it had grown so accustomed to. This took time and, yep, more goddamn patience.

With Dr. McHale, the first step was to understand my body, the adrenal glands (which I'd never heard of), the brain and the gut, and how they all interplay. Again, it's important not think of your mind and your body as completely separate and independent entities; there is no single part of your body that does not, in some way, connect with another. The sooner you embrace the mind and body's inextricable link, the better you will feel in all aspects of your well-being.

To bring it back to our brain chemistry, which we touched on in Chapter 1, she explained:

> When we want to understand anxiety and panic disorder from a physiological perspective, it is important to consider the role of our neurotransmitters (chemical signals within the nervous system; e.g., brain, spinal cord and nerves

throughout our bodies) that send messages from one nerve to another across a gap between the nerves (which is known scientifically as the "synaptic cleft") or from a nerve to a target cell (such as telling the cell to repair). Our nerves do not physically touch one another, so the neurotransmitter sends the message from one nerve ending to another in chemical form to exert a change—or to send a signal to the next nerve almost like a row of dominos—both of which are chemical messengers in the body, i.e., messages sent from one place to another.

If that's all a bit much to digest, the easiest way to get your head around neurotransmitters is to think of them like text messages; simple instructions from one part of the body to tell another part what to do. What we don't want is for those messages to misfire or arrive in some form of gobbledygook language.

In Chapter 1, we covered the role of the amygdala, the part of the brain that processes emotion. When we perceive a stress or a threat, the amygdala sends a text message—via a neurotransmitter—to the command center of the brain to activate the autonomic nervous system that governs involuntary responses in organs like the heart, lungs, eyes, etc. Neurotransmitters act super fast, sending messages within a matter of milliseconds, while the actual hormones take a little bit longer to register.

Still with me? Good.

When the body is in distress the sympathetic nervous system (the fight-or-flight bit, not its friendlier, rest-and-digest counterpart) is triggered via the autonomic nerves that travel to the adrenal glands. They're part of the endocrine/hormonal system of the body, and sit atop the kidney on both the right and left sides of your body. The adrenal glands then secrete the hormone adrenaline, which is released into our blood to send messages of distress around the body so that we can effectively survive the perceived threat. Similarly, signals are sent from the hypothalamus in the brain, to the pituitary gland and on to the adrenal gland instructing the adrenal gland to make another stress hormone that most people will be familiar with—and I've mentioned it a *lot*—cortisol (in the cortex of the adrenal gland). At this point, the diagram on page 162 should be making a little bit more sense.

Cortisol is a longer-acting stress hormone compared to adrenaline, which is why it's the one we need to tame over time. Much like adrenaline, cortisol enables us to cope with stress by increasing our blood sugar, and therefore energy (driving the sugar to our muscles and our brain to address the stressful situation), suppressing our immune system (which is why prolonged stress gives us all kinds of immune dysfunction), focus, concentration and memory, etc. The short-term release of cortisol is beneficial—and essential for our survival—but long-term frequent release makes us feel like sh*t.

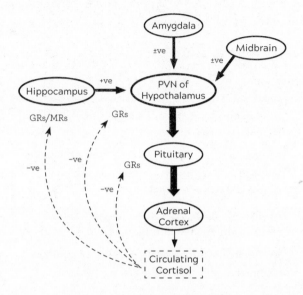

When taking our diet into consideration, we need to:

· Eat the right foods to ensure that all of these little players are functioning optimally.

· Focus on low GI foods vs. high GI foods.

· Strengthen our adrenal glands (the maker of hormones) so they're not producing unhelpful and unhealthy hormones.

· Reduce the long-term production of cortisol (because, remember, if we overproduce cortisol, we don't give the sleep hormone, melatonin, a fighting chance).

- Increase our feel-good neurotransmitters serotonin (the "happy hormone" responsible for feelings of well-being) and GABA (another goodie—an inhibitory neurotransmitter).

Behold, Dr. McHale's rules of thumb for an anti-anxiety diet:

- When you are feeling anxious, avoid adding fuel to the fire and steer clear of simple sugars like candy, chocolate cakes, bread, etc.

- Excessive cortisol production will lead to higher bloodsugar levels so you really don't need to make things worse for yourself.

- Avoid caffeine as it's a stimulant, and you don't need any brain stimulation.

- Avoid alcohol during acute periods of anxiety. Hangovers will make things worse.

Remember that all carbohydrates break down into sugar, but what you want to be mindful of is the "simple sugars" or "processed carbohydrates." These aren't ideal for three reasons:

1. They don't tend to be nutrient-dense, so they're of no real health value.

2. Processed foods don't sit well with the gut (more on this later).

3. These foods tend to release glucose very quickly into the body, resulting in a spike in stress hormones.

Instead, opt for foods with a lower glycemic index (GI), which is a measure of the amount of carbohydrates in food and their impact on our blood-sugar levels. Oats in the evening are a fantastic example. Low GI foods release energy into the body at a slower rate, meaning you avoid those nasty spikes of sugar that increase heart rate, etc. Generally, foods with a high GI are not as good for you.

High GI carbohydrates will increase the level of stress hormones—albeit temporarily—in and of themselves, so having gone through the mechanisms of the stress response above, you can see why that is not wise.

Below is a list showing foods with a high GI vs. foods with a low GI (that you should try to eat instead).

White bread	VS	Rye bread
Potatoes, corn, carrots, beets, turnips, parsnips	VS	All other vegetables (green leafy vegetables have a particularly low GI rating)
Bananas, melons, pineapple, raisins	VS	All other fruits
Chips	VS	Nuts (peanut butter–not full of sugar or palm oil–is a great low GI snack)
Cornflakes	VS	Muesli
Pasta	VS	Vermicelli rice noodles

High GI foods can cause a very sharp elevation in stress hormone levels, prompting an even sharper decline, which can lead to major problems with mood, irritability and coping strategies.

Eat plenty of dark green veggies. But don't go nuts on veg either; everything in moderation. Too much or too little of anything can give rise to other problems we hadn't planned on, such as problems in your gut.

Ensuring optimal vitamin and mineral levels is absolutely essential. B vitamins (particularly vitamin B6), vitamin C, magnesium, and tryptophan are crucial to the metabolic pathways involved in neurotransmitter synthesis and adrenal-gland health. Testing is advised because on one hand, an anxious person deficient in magnesium may sleep better, on the other, if someone already has optimal levels of magnesium, an added supplement will do nothing other than give them diarrhea.

One of the best ways to support your adrenal glands is with sleep—so head to Chapter 15 if you're reading this at 3 AM.

Remember that everything is working in tandem. A low-GI carbohydrate or a vitamin D supplement isn't going to stop a panic attack. However, food and supplements (if necessary), when taken regularly alongside exercise and meditation (and other lifestyle interventions) gives us the opportunity to build a healthy, strong body and more resilient mind.

Optimizing gut function is paramount. There is ample research surrounding the link between the gut and the brain, but the terminology is very complex and quite the head scratcher. Quite simply, there exists a bidirectional communication network between the gut and the brain. In fact, the gut is often referred to as the second brain. The brain affects the gut but the gut affects the brain, too, and thus our thoughts, feelings, and behaviors.

So while you're making efforts with CBT to stop any wobbles in your tummy, you can also optimize your gut health so that it improves your mood. This link occurs via what's called the vagus nerve, and the system has been dubbed the gut-brain axis. What's more, research suggests that serotonin plays a crucial role in this communication system since the majority—90 percent—of our serotonin is actually produced in the gut. The "second brain" label derives from the gut's ability to operate autonomously and communicate with the central nervous system (both sympathetic and parasympathetic). Quite literally, the emotional and cognitive centers of our brains are linked with some intestinal functions, which is why you feel stress in your digestive system.

The key here is the serotonin and the balance of good gut bacteria; there is strong evidence that gut micro-organisms can activate the vagus nerve and play a critical role in mediating effects on the brain and behavior. Our gut microbiota (the human microbiota includes bacteria, fungi, viruses) influences our production of serotonin and dopamine. Just as serotonin is essential for our mood, it's also a huge factor in gastrointestinal motility.

How to optimize your gut? Follow a nutritious diet, ensuring you eat lots of vegetables and avoid processed foods. Processed foods and some dairy produce should also be avoided for gut issues as they are common gut irritants. It's also often recommended that you add fermented foods (a good natural probiotic) into the mix but, again, I would get the advice of a professional. Probiotic supplements are also a fantastic option, but this is best done after having your own microbiome (the genetic makeup of the bacteria, fungi and viruses that make up the microbiota) tested. This testing of the gut function will detect any other unhelpful organisms that should be gotten rid of, and will clarify exactly what the right microbial strain and dosage is for you.

What you should know about exercise

EXERCISE IS ANOTHER crucial element in the management of anxiety, but what I *didn't* know, and what you might not know either, is that it can also sometimes be a contributing factor, or at least worsen what you're already experiencing.

Before I freak you out and turn you into a couch potato forever more, which wouldn't be a good idea, let me explain, with the help of Dr. McHale.

During my acute anxiety phase, the most rational thing I could think to do was just run until I no longer felt anxious. I wanted to run away from it—in every sense of the word—so I ran fast and hard until I had no breath left. But then I started to notice that the more I ran, over the course of days and weeks, the more anxious I felt. Was I allergic to exercise now, too? No, but I didn't understand how different exercise affects our hormones and, as we now know, hormones are crucial contenders as far as anxiety is concerned. What I also didn't realize was how certain exercises are better suited to certain people. It turns out that running is just not for me. Dr. McHale explains:

> It's important to be mindful that exercise is a stress on the body. Most forms of exercise stimulate cortisol production. And to be clear, that stress can be highly beneficial, but also extremely detrimental. So, in particular with an individual who suffers from anxiety or panic attacks, given all we have learned to this point about what happens physiologically and biochemically when we experience anxiety and panic, any *further* stress on the body must be carefully monitored. We want to reduce cortisol, not increase it.

It makes sense, right? If you're already hugely stressed out, and you pump more of the same stress hormones around your body, it's bound to cause a spike. For this reason, I turned to yoga, primarily for the fact that certain forms tend to be not as stressful on the body and actually stimulate the parasympathetic nervous system, thanks to its dependency on slow, controled breaths.

Dr. McHale's thoughts on yoga:

> It's a fantastic form of activity. In terms of anxiety, I would recommend everyone to try some form of yoga (though for acute anxiety I would steer away from Bikram/hot yoga; it's too intense) because of the exceptional benefits you can derive, mainly due to the activation of the parasympathetic nervous system.

Some yoga poses for relieving anxiety

Below are some pose names; look up a quick "how-to" on YouTube and get in the habit of trying these when you feel you need it.

1. Child's Pose (Balasana): I love that this counts as exercise
2. Tree Pose (Vriksasana)
3. Warrior III (Virabhadrasana III)
4. Legs Up the Wall Pose (Viparita Karani): My all-time favorite anti-anxiety pose that literally flips your perspective!

If you really get into it, *Yoga Journal* online (yogajournal.com) has countless other poses that help you get your bliss on.

So, why didn't running bode well with me at the time?

Dr. McHale says:

> I suggested avoiding steady-pace running for
> you, partly because you are slight and have very
> low levels of body fat. Neither would steady-pace
> cardio, like running, give you the best results in
> terms of the therapeutic effect. Individuals with
> very low body fat levels with very little muscle mass
> tend toward having less estrogen, which is linked
> with higher than average cortisol levels.
>
> Similarly, given your personal set of
> circumstances, I felt that moderate/mild weight
> training would be more beneficial in terms of
> cortisol management, which was key for you.

Weight training is currently widely accepted to be of benefit to most people. It's often recommended to those who suffer from anxiety or panic for not only the general benefits but because it is measurable and controlled in terms of intensity and recovery, etc. Though more research in this area is needed, weight training tends to result in greater symptomatic improvement in less time than is the case with steady-pace cardio, and this seems to be directly linked to its effect on cortisol.

Remember though that resistance training doesn't just mean actual dumbbells and barbells, it also includes bodyweight exercises, kettlebells, TRX, and so on and so forth.

So there, I found my winning combination of exercise for mental health—a little bit of yoga and a realiztic amount of resistance training (which for me was some bodyweight training and some training with extra weights). Not that I wouldn't rather eat a pack of Oreos on the couch, any day.

As with diet, you're really best off with a tailor-made program to suit your specific goals. Dr. McHale suggests three twenty-minute planned exercise sessions per week at a maximum:

> But, most importantly, just aim to be a little bit more active in everyday life. Using a step tracker is extremely useful; try aiming for 10,000 steps per day: walk to the shop, take the stairs, get off the bus a few stops earlier on the way to work.
>
> Exercise is just movement. But the very word "exercise" holds negative connotations for far too many people. Some people instantly think "gym," "heavy weights," "Arnold Schwarzenegger-types," and this leads to nothing but dread and even more anxiety.

Other people have equally negative feelings about running outside. Then, there are those who despise cycling or hill-walking or even going for a stroll with the dog. The reality is that they are *all* generally beneficial (from a mental health perspective). In various reports, you will find claims that cardio exercise (running, etc.)

is scientifically better for anxiety or weight training is better for depression (and maybe, the next day, it will say weight training is *not* wise for depression). Some research will show that high intensity interval training (HIIT) is bad for those suffering from anxiety disorder and other findings will show steady pace cardio is not advisable for depression, etc.

First and foremost, try to find a form of activity that you enjoy. Find something that you will look forward to doing regularly and that you know will make you feel good.

Second, when choosing your preferred exercise to help in the management of anxiety, think more about the therapeutic effects of exercising rather than its fat-burning ability. This is your focus right now.

Also remember that even for the person who absolutely lives for training, whatever the discipline itself may be, there are days where even they just don't feel like doing anything. That is normal, so don't beat yourself up over that and definitely don't give up. Just because one day you didn't feel up to going doesn't mean it's not for you. *Nobody* is bouncing out of the house to go for a walk or go to the gym every single hour of every single day.

On those days when you don't really feel like moving, it helps to have a mental list of things you ask yourself:

- Are you exhausted? Have you just overdone it this week and do you genuinely need a rest?

- Are you being lazy? And be honest (we all genuinely know the answer ourselves).

- How do you think you will feel after you exercise?

- How did you feel the last time you didn't really feel like working out, but you went anyway?

Some final words from Dr. McHale:

> Remember there's no harm in at least going for a little while and seeing how you feel, especially if you already planned the time in your day to go. If you're really not up to it when you're there and in the swing of it, then just leave! At least then you tried. Very rarely do people start exercising and not actually feel the benefit.

So what'll it be for you?

Understanding the science behind why resistance training and yoga were more helpful to me than cardio has, to this day, been one of my greatest discoveries in my quest to own my anxiety. But, for you, running might be your biggest anxiety-reliever. Again, there's no one-size-fits-all guide.

If you don't feel good doing an exercise, is it because it's producing more cortisol in your body (if you don't think you'd know, don't worry—you'll feel it), so you feel more intermittently anxious, or is it because you just think it's a crap class? Whatever the reason, just try something else.

 **Chapter Summary**

- *Exercise is an essential aspect of anxiety management and should not be overlooked.*

- *Countless studies continue to prove the positive impact that exercise has on our mental health and sense of wellbeing in general.*

- *Find the exercise that makes you feel good; enjoying an activity—whatever you choose—is crucial. If you hate it, it might just contribute to your feelings of anxiety.*

- *Be mindful of high-intensity cardio when you are in an intense period of anxiety; something more complementary to your parasympathetic system, such as yoga, may suit your body better and help to calm things down.*

Let's talk about meds

MEDICATION. LET'S TALK medication. (Treads very carefully.)

Within the realm of mental health, medication has always been a touchy subject—and I get it. Understandably, there's a fear that those suffering with anxiety would turn to medication in a heartbeat without addressing the root cause of the problem. This is a valid concern, but if you've been keeping up with me thus far, you'll know that I'm *all* about addressing the problem in its entirety, rather than simply slapping a bandage on the boo-boo and hoping it just goes away.

Your anxiety won't improve if you don't take time to assess and address why it's happening—it just won't. Having said that, there's a significant and unfair stigma attached to mental health medication that, in my view, perpetuates the problem. In my own personal experience, medication was a significant factor in my recovery and if I didn't discuss it in this book, I'd not be telling you the whole truth. Simply put, it helped me claw my way out of the ditch and get back on an even keel—on a hormonal level—which, in turn, enabled me to then benefit from all my other approaches, such as mindfulness, yoga and breathing exercises.

You see, anxiety is a vicious cycle (or two-way street) that affects us on two distinct levels. We know that destructive thoughts can have an effect on your physiology but, equally so, an out of whack physiology (i.e., if your endocrine system is out of commission for a period of time, because you've been under mounting stress in work) can have an effect on your thought processes. Yep, it's a real bitch. But, in a way, it gives you two clear things to treat: your thought processes and your physical symptoms. For me, medication helped me to tackle the latter, which, conveniently, improved the former.

It depends on the severity of your anxiety, of course, and this is something you absolutely need to discuss with your doctor. But here's how it went for me.

I was suffering with acute, crippling, and physical anxiety for an extended period of time. I was ill. Because I hadn't recognized the symptoms and was completely in the dark about why I was feeling the way I did, my anxiety brought me to a place that, at the time, I thought was the point of no return.

In retrospect, had I understood the situation and saved myself from freaking out, I might not ever have needed medication. My hope is that you're reading this book in time and you'll bounce back without it, but don't worry if you don't. I didn't. I hit rock bottom. My hormones were all over the place and, try as I might, I just couldn't get my head above water through sheer willpower alone and the breathing exercises just weren't doing it for me.

I needed some industrial-strength intervention. I wasn't sleeping, I wasn't eating and I was in physical pain from the tension—not to mention trying to deal with the severity of my panic.

I spent more time crying than not crying. I questioned whether or not I'd ever feel like me again, as well as pondering the possibility of making it all go away, for good. (This thought still makes me feel very sad, but here's what I do: I visualize myself *now* going back to myself *then* and I wrap my arms tightly around myself. It works.)

That was the point at which I knew I needed help. I needed the kind of lift that a walk in fresh air just couldn't give me.

The thing is, I felt so bad about myself for going on medication that this contributed further to my own suffering. I, myself, was participating in the stigma by deciding that taking medication meant I wasn't strong enough or that I was weak, and I was embarrassed to say I needed it. Even to this day, though I try to practice what I preach by normalizing it among friends and family (and even people I don't know) so that the stigma will eventually just f*ck off on the horse it rode in on, I still squirm internally when, for example, I'm filling out a form and have to admit that I'm on medication for my—cue thriller movie music—brain.

Sometimes, people seem genuinely shocked that I'm on medication, and I try to dumb it down and justify it by saying, "Well, I'm on a really light dosage because I was very physically ill and I'm going to come off it any day now because I'm doing really great," etc. But, feel free to share this sentiment: f*ck that.

Nobody, not one person, has the right to judge you, however the hell you come out the other side—and *you will*. They're not feeling it, you are, and it's the f*cking WORST.

If I was physically unwell with a kidney infection or a broken leg, there would be no questioning my need for medication and nobody would look at me sideways and I just wouldn't feel that tiny pit of shame in my stomach. But for some bizarre reason—perhaps it's our collective fear of admitting our vulnerability—we're still not there in terms of speaking about medication and mental health. We tend to think of physical problems as something that's been thrust upon us, something that we've no control over or something that's just happened to us. With mental health, it's a different story. It's seen as something we *can* control, something we can decide on and something that—if you've got a problem—you're doing to yourself, so, maybe, y'know, you should just stop. Dear reader, this is horsesh*t.

I really didn't want to feel the way I felt. Last time I checked, I didn't possess any masochistic tendencies, and I'm going to go right ahead and assume that you don't either. I tried so very hard to "snap out of it" (oh yes, why didn't I think of that? What brilliant advice!) and questioned why I couldn't just feel better or be happy when, on paper, I'd had a pretty fantastic life. But to reiterate, because this cannot be reiterated enough, anxiety is a physiological experience that while strongly linked with your thought processes, can have a very physical manifestation. It's not just something we think, it's something we feel. And this one's a major bugbear of mine: It's not just "all in your head."

In fact, feel free to kick anyone who says this square in the balls. I grant you permission. Assholes.

So, back to my medication. I decided, with the support of my nearest and dearest, that medication was a choice I wanted to make. Why force myself to go it alone? Why punish myself any minute longer after months of pure turmoil out of fear of what this might say about me or what people would think of me? Instead of thinking of it as a quick fix—it wasn't—or something that would just let me completely off the hook so I didn't have to do any work myself—it didn't—I decided it was a brave move. I was accepting my vulnerability, I was taking action and I was going to do whatever it took to save myself.

The thing about long-term anti-anxiety medication (and not just a fast-acting, short-term benzodiazepine, for example) is that it can be tricky to find one that works for you. You don't take one tablet and wake up the next morning with a burning desire to go bungee jumping. Even if you do manage to hit the nail on the head on your first try, the first six weeks can be pretty unforgiving (which, ironically, is a good sign in the long run). It's not yet understood precisely why it can take this many weeks to adjust, but just know that if that's how long it takes you, it's normal.

Here's how they work. There are different long-term medications on the market. Most commonly, you'd be prescribed an **SSRI**, which is a selective serotonin reuptake inhibitor—e.g., Prozac, Lexapro, Zoloft—or an **SNRI**, which stands for selective serotonin and noradrenaline reuptake inhibitor. You might also have heard of beta blockers, tricyclics and other forms of anti-anxiety medication, but the former are the most common.

These medications serve to balance our neurotransmitters and, in most cases, given that we anxiety-sufferers tend to be low on serotonin, they encourage the production of more serotonin. SSRIs block (inhibit) serotonin from being reabsorbed (reuptake) back into the nerve cells they came from, because nerves typically recycle these neurotransmitters.

We don't want that. This leads to an increased concentration of serotonin in the synaptic cleft—the space between the two communicating cells (remember, we ventured there in Chapter 17). Research shows and scientists believe that all of this extra serotonin can then strengthen communication between the nerve cells, specifically the circuits associated with mood regulation. Traditionally, SSRIs were prescribed for depression, but, today, they are commonly used for their ability to balance the hormonal players involved in anxiety.

Then, there are your quick fixes.

Benzodiazepines should only ever be used in short-term critical situations; this kind of medication is highly addictive, so long-term use is absolutely not recommended. This type of medication—Xanax being the most popular—is highly effective in alleviating acute severe episodes of panic. They exert their anxiolytic (anti-anxiety) effect by enhancing the action of GABA, which is our inhibitory neurotransmitter. They take effect, which results in sedative, hypnotic (sleep-inducing) and muscle relaxant properties, within about twenty minutes.

Anti-anxiety medication isn't the only option, but it *is* an option, and one that you have every right to consider. My only stipulation is that you do it under the guidance of an understanding doctor (well, you have to; legally, that is) that you monitor your progress carefully, ensuring it's agreeing with you, and that you still ensure to address your situation and the root of your anxiety, as well as keeping on top of your daily maintenance.

Sometimes, I wrongly credit my choice to go on medication as the sole reason I've bounced back. This isn't true. As I'd intended, it simply helped to take the sting out of the physical symptoms that had kept me under my duvet, enabling me to feel well enough for long enough so that I *could* benefit from my other endeavors, one of which was CBT (see Chapter 16).

As I said at the outset of this book, it's rarely a case of choosing one way out and sticking with it; it'll no doubt be a combination of things that will ultimately contribute to your newfound wellness. It certainly was for me.

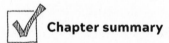 **Chapter summary**

- *Medication is an option worth discussing with your GP if your anxiety is chronic and acute.*

- *Lifestyle changes come first. Don't turn to medication without addressing all aspects of your anxiety and making the necessary changes once you've identified why you are feeling this way.*

- *Medication can be very effective when it comes to balancing the hormones involved with anxiety, but you shouldn't treat it as a bandage without looking at the root cause.*

- *If you need to, you shouldn't feel less than for turning to medication. It is not a cop-out. Taking positive action to get yourself feeling good again is brave.*

- *Turning to medication does not mean the work is done. Medication, if you take it, is just one aspect of your owning it.*

CHAPTER 20

Ass-kicking alternative therapies and treatments

YOU COULD WRITE an entire book dedicated to each and every alternative (and by "alternative" I mean nontraditional in Western medicine) anti-anxiety treatment available to you. But, here, I will home in on what worked for me and what didn't so you can do the same.

As with everything else in this book, it's never going to be one thing alone that makes the difference; it's the coming together of all your efforts with CBT, exercise, diet, one or several alternative treatment modalities and, depending on the severity of your anxiety, medication could well play its part, too. One mistake I kept making was in thinking that one session of this or that would "cure" me. I'd walk into a therapist's office or a physical treatment room, for acupuncture or hypnotherapy, expecting to emerge as a new person, and that was an awful lot of pressure to place on one experience—and on myself. I so wanted to believe that "one session is all it takes" and that I'd never feel stressed again. But please, do yourself a favor, and approach every treatment with a healthy dose of caution. I would have handed over a thousand bucks to a goat if it told me it could help.

The common theme with all the treatment options I list in this chapter is that they serve to relax you, physically and mentally, so, naturally, you will walk away from one session feeling a little bit more mellow than when you came in.

This is good, but it doesn't mean that your anxiety is gone, healed by some higher being, never to return—which is why I'd wind up ten times more frustrated when, a few days later, I'd feel anxious all over again. The point here is to find a treatment option that you like, that makes you feel good, and give yourself a fair few sessions to get your body used to this state of deep relaxation, taking you out of any acutely sensitive period, so that you can then benefit from the things you can do yourself, such as mindfulness or your breathing exercises.

When you do get to a point of owning your anxiety, know that it's *you* and your combined efforts that have got you to this point; giving all the credit to one alternative treatment that magically realigned your chakras would be doing yourself a massive disservice.

When I was feeling particularly bad, I was vulnerable as hell and therefore willing to believe anyone who promised to make me feel better. It's very easy to get caught up in things like chakras or auras and angels, and it's very easy to believe that there's some higher power or magical force at work. It's really important that you take ownership of your anxiety in this way, otherwise we perpetuate the idea that anxiety is some foreign entity, over which we ourselves have no control, and that it can only be got rid of by something equally benign and powerful.

Bullsh*t.

You are powerful, anxiety is not.

Bring everything back down to Earth and focus on the cold, hard physiological effects that a given treatment can have on your body and you will cut out all of the BS, I promise. These things help, and they can help hugely, but they are not the sole answer to your struggles. Essentially, where these treatments work well is when you're feeling very overwhelmed by your seemingly insurmountable anxiety and you need the expertise of someone else to guide you toward a point of relaxation. Even before you begin your treatment, just knowing that you're in the company of someone who understands, someone onto whom you can offload some of your worries, is already a positive experience. Again, as with your CBT therapist, be sure to find an alternative therapist that you like being in the company of; the connection with the person healing you is just as important as the treatment itself.

Now, so as not to offend anyone who does buy into the kind of healing I've referenced above, if it works for you, and you get some relief from it, then that's all that matters. Keep doing it.

For me, though, I bring it back to what was happening inside my body. When I'm anxious, my alarm system (amygdala) is firing off willy-nilly, producing stress hormones (cortisol and adrenaline) that make me feel like crap, and, eventually, they tire out my more advanced brain (prefrontal cortex) that has become so overworked by stress that all my thoughts become tinged with fear, and this, in turn, causes my body to produce more physical symptoms of anxiety.

If I engage in an activity (such as one of the treatments you're going to read about in this chapter) that helps to calm down the physical symptoms, I will calm down my entire system, the stress hormones will retreat and, in time, my anxious thoughts will be replaced by more rational thinking. But this takes time and a lot of patience, and it's also something you have to do consistently, spending as much time as possible with your body feeling physically relaxed.

Don't underestimate the powerful links between that which we feel mentally and that which we feel physically.

The key to alternative treatments and anxiety is to find something that relaxes you deeply to engage the parasympathetic nervous system, so that when we have the treatment regularly, you soothe the sympathetic nervous system (the stress response), desensitizing your brain to fearful thoughts, external and internal stimuli. In this way, you gain control of your anxiety.

Bioenergy healing

I was intrigued to try bio-energy healing and I quite enjoyed my sessions. However, some might argue that it would indeed fall under the new-agey-mumbo-jumbo category—having said that, it's been practiced for thousands of years in several cultures, so new-age it is not.

While those who are qualified to perform it will believe that a higher force delivers healing through their hands to your body and mind—and there's nothing wrong with that if you do believe it—I simply benefited from the state of deep relaxation that gentle touch to the body can yield. That's it.

For a treatment, you lie down, warm blankets are placed over you (because when our bodies relax our temperature tends to drop, it's the same reason we need duvets at night), and a guided audio meditation with soothing music is played as your therapist applies long gentle strokes over your face, arms, legs, feet, and stomach.

The belief here is that the therapist is channeling life-force energy to the client to help clear, charge and energize their body's energy fields. Also relevant to this alternative treatment is the idea of "vibrations." When we are healthy and anxiety-free, every cell and organ in our body is said to be vibrating at its optimum frequency, but when we are sick (mentally or physically), our vibration frequency has gone awry.

Whether you get on board with these ideas or not doesn't really matter, you just need to think of it as a very soothing, very calming experience through which you will feel deeply relaxed—it was definitely among the most relaxing treatments I've had—and any period of deep relaxation is worth it when you've been suffering with anxiety to help your nervous system rebalance.

Enjoy it for what it is, and don't expect it to change your life in one go; it merely gives you a break from feeling like crap and it gives your recovery (from a point of acute anxiety) a helping hand.

Havening (Amygdala Depotentiation Therapy)

Havening (pronounced like a "safe *haven*") is similar to bioenergy healing (in terms of physical touch) but arguably more sophisticated. It's a relatively new treatment that I found to be very effective, particularly when it comes to specific fears or phobias.

Unlike plenty of other "alternative" treatments, havening is impressively rooted in neuroscience, meaning any initial skepticism is appeased quickly. I spoke to Stephen Travers, one of the foremost certified havening practitioners in the world, who explained how the latest breakthrough in psychological therapy works:

> Havening is a psychosensory therapy, which means it uses pleasant psychological distraction techniques and relaxing touch, which can be applied by the therapist or by the clients themselves. The treatment itself is very calming, comforting and relaxing. It affects the amygdala, which controls your stress response. Havening switches off the signals from the brain that cause emotional and physical distress. These powerful healing results can often be achieved within minutes and last a lifetime, which makes it an extraordinary therapy.

Founded by medical doctor and neuroscientist Dr. Ronald Ruden,[13] we now have an insight into the ways in which traumatic memories become encoded in the brain and precisely where this happens: the lateral amygdala. From this breakthrough, Dr. Ruden then worked out how to remove the emotional and distressful symptoms from the memory or trauma, which led him to this psychosensory therapy. Also known as Amygdala Depotentiation Therapy, Dr. Ruden's work has been hailed by many of his peers as one of the most significant breakthroughs in the fields of psychology and neuroscience. I like it because it's simple, it makes complete sense and, for me, it was effective.

From my guinea-pig perspective, it's totally unlike talking therapy or anything else I've tried; rather than just sitting there chronicling the myriad ways in which I felt I was struggling, with no real changes occurring in my brain, I got straight to work replacing what was set in my mind as a negative, stressful feeling with something that was relaxed and content, all via the sensory touch of my practitioner.

This touch sends the loveliest delta waves to your brain, meaning that when you then go back to think about what it was that set you off in the first place, you don't feel it in the same way. There's also lots of distraction techniques involved, which, at first, might seem ridiculous—I think at one point I was humming "Old MacDonald Had a Farm"—but are very effective in terms of interrupting those negative thought patterns we find lodged in our brain chemistry. The most common issues presented at a havening session are those relating to anxiety and stress, and with more and more people, both clients and medical professionals, turning their heads toward this treatment, it's soon to go fully mainstream.

After two sessions, I felt more relaxed and less affected by bad memories, as well as enjoying a confidence boost.

With thousands of completed case studies and the first published paper on the benefits of havening via King's College in London,[14] this is a side-effect-free anxiety treatment that gets my vote.

Sound therapy

This is another option that I have great faith in, primarily because of how it gets right to the physical job of balancing our parasympathetic nervous system (relaxation response) with our sympathetic nervous system (stress response), and desensitizes our minds and bodies.

As I've explained before, when we're anxious, it's the stress response that's in the driving seat and the parasympathetic nervous system is heavily outweighed by the former. Sound therapy also respects the reality that given how anxiety is fueled by the autonomic fight-or-flight response, it's not as simple as telling it to just calm down. This awareness is so important. You have to soothe it indirectly and you do this by training and conditioning your brain.

Beyond the crucial CBT, one such way to condition your brain positively—think of it as Herbal Essences for the inside of your head—is with sound therapy. Sound therapy originates from ancient times when shamans beat their drums not only to enter into altered states of consciousness—you know, when you're so relaxed or hypnotized by a soothing rhythm or sound that you feel as though you're somewhere else entirely—but also to offer healing to their people. From the Australian Aboriginals' didgeridoo to the Roman Aulus Cornelius Celsus who was a big fan of the sound of cymbals and running water for the treatment of mental disorders, sound and sound vibrations have been used from ancient times as a successful therapy by tweaking the brain's activity.

Today, we know that a rhythmic sound has the power to alter our brainwave patterns, driving the mind into a relaxed or even a deep meditative state. Sound therapy can help you alleviate anxiety by retraining your brain to relax, ultimately calming down your fight-or-flight response and nurturing your relaxation response. Very simply, through sound therapy, you are going to lower your general anxiety levels and you will retrain your parasympathetic system by empowering your relaxation response. But, like everything else, this is something you'll want to be doing regularly so that your relaxation response can really take the lead.

Mindfulness courses

Mindfulness, of course, is something we can and should be doing every day, weaving it into our lives so that it becomes as much a part of our routine as sleeping or eating, but if you find yourself right in the midst of a bad bout of anxiety, it can be incredibly worthwhile to sign up for a more intensive mindfulness course, where your chances of being distracted by social media or bottles of Prosecco in your fridge will be limited.

Undertaking mindfulness with groups of other people has also proven to be particularly helpful. It just makes it a whole lot easier to get in the zone and it takes a lot of the stress out of "trying" to practice mindfulness on your own when you can just follow the guidance of someone in front of you. If you can't get to a real-life mindfulness course, download some apps, such as Headspace, Calm, and Stop, Breathe & Think, so that you have three great options with which to mix it up (this is something you're ideally going to be doing every day, so if you listen to the same guide day in, day out, you'll get fed up and you'll give up). These are my three favorites, but there are plenty of decent mindfulness apps on the market. You can download meditations also on mindfulness-solution.com, which comes recommended by Harvard University.

Quite simply, the process involves sitting or lying comfortably, focusing on your breathing, and then bringing your mind's attention to the present without drifting into concerns about the past or future. Sometimes, there will be counting involved (in your head) or other subtle ways to keep your mind focused.

Unfortunately though, when it comes to studies to back up the benefits associated with mindfulness, it can be hard to find unbiased reports. The thing is, when researchers are looking for people to participate in a study, chances are they're already pro-mindfulness and will report only positive results. Really what's needed—the same as all studies—is a solid control group.

Saving me heaps of time, researchers from Johns Hopkins University in Baltimore, MD, sifted through nearly 19,000 meditation studies, finding forty-seven trials that addressed this exact set of issues, satisfactorily meeting their criteria for well-designed studies. And their findings are hard to argue with. If you're not yet gone on the idea, you can read all about their straight-up, no-frills findings in The JAMA Network online (the study is called "Meditation Programs for Psychological Stress and Wellbeing: A Systematic Review and Meta-Analysis").[15] In short, their review of all the other reviews found unanimous evidence of the positive impact of mindfulness meditation on participants.

They conclude that mindfulness is not going to change your life dramatically in one go, but that clinicians (and us mere mortals) should be open-minded about the fact that mindfulness meditation programs absolutely lead to moderate improvements in anxiety. For you, it might drastically improve your symptoms over time. I hope it does. For me, it was certainly a major contributing factor to my ability to "own it," but where I fell down initially was in my impatience and unwillingness to keep at it daily. When done in tandem with everything else, it works. Even on a short-term basis, I certainly have never finished a session of mindfulness and felt anxious, not even when I've been particularly bad, so there's just no good reason not to try it.

Commenting on the physical effects of mindfulness on the brain, Dr. Coyne says:

> Neuroscientists have shown that practicing mindfulness affects brain areas related to perception, body awareness, pain tolerance, emotion regulation, introspection, complex thinking and sense of self. While more research is needed to document these changes over time and to understand exactly why, the evidence is compelling. World-renowned neuroscientist Richie Davidson at the Center for Healthy Minds at the University of Wisconsin-Madison,[16] along with his colleagues, wants us to know three things:
>
> · You can train your brain to change.
>
> · The change is measurable.
>
> · New ways of thinking can change it for the better.

There are a number of ways your brain may change when you practice mindfulness:

· Increased gray matter changes have been noted in the anterior cingulate cortex (ACC), which is a structure located behind the brain's frontal lobe. It has been associated with attention-related, self-regulatory processes, which enables more cognitive flexibility.

- Increased grey matter density was also found in areas of the prefrontal lobe, which are primarily responsible for executive functioning, such as planning, problem-solving and emotion regulation.

- Increased cortical thickness in the hippocampus has also been noted. The hippocampus is the part of the limbic system that governs learning and memory, and is extraordinarily susceptible to stress and stress-related disorders like depression or PTSD.

- Studies have also shown that the amygdala, our brain's alarm system controling our fight-or-flight response, decreases in brain cell volume after mindfulness practice.

- Not only does the amygdala shrink post-mindfulness practice, but the functional connections between the amygdala and the prefrontal cortex are weakened. This causes less reactivity, and also paves the way for connections between areas associated with higher-order brain functions to be strengthened (i.e., attention, concentration, etc.).

Exercise
S.T.O.P. MINDFULNESS

Creating space in your day to S.T.O.P. and get back into the present is enormously helpful in alleviating the negative effects of our stress response. When we drop into the present, we are more likely to gain perspective, create a space between thoughts, feelings, and behavior, and make wiser decisions and kinder choices for ourselves.

Here's a short practice you can weave into your day to check your mental weather:

- STOP what you're doing. Put everything down for a minute.
- TAKE a few deep breaths.
- OBSERVE your experience just as it is. Reconnect with your feelings and thoughts. Don't judge them. Check in with how your body feels. What do you need right now?
- PROCEED with something that will nourish you in the moment.

Get curious about when there are opportunities in the day for you to just S.T.O.P. (e.g., waking up, taking a shower, before eating a meal, at a traffic light, at work). What would it be like in the days, weeks, and months ahead if you started S.T.O.P.ping more often?

Acupuncture

Last but by no means least, when it came to the physical symptoms of anxiety—the aches and pains in the mornings, the sleeplessness, and all other physical nastiness—I turned to acupuncture, for which I still, to this day, have fairly regular treatments.

Essentially, by inserting painless needles at specific points in the body, acupuncturists can effect actual chemical changes in parts of the brain to reduce anxiety and make long-term changes.

Because acupuncture and traditional Chinese medicine hails from the East, many Westerners have been stereotypically quick to demerit it in the face of the Western medicine with which we are more familiar. For some, the idea of sticking needles in your skin does sound like pure bullsh*t, but as someone with a strong bullsh*t detector, rest assured that this is a treatment option that's heavily supported by scientific studies. What's more, across the globe, acupuncture is gaining traction within the conventional medical field in the form of its acceptance as an adjunct treatment in hospitals and clinics. It appears in cancer care, emergency medicine, and maternity and fertility clinics across the USA, Australia, New Zealand, and Europe.

So, when it comes to anxiety in particular, you don't have to choose Western or Eastern treatments alone; they can complement each other beautifully and, for me, given that I also went down the route of medication, acupuncture was a perfect addition. I slept like a baby after each session and it massively improved my physical symptoms.

To explain how acupuncture works with anxiety, I've recruited the help of Hannah O'Connell, my acupuncturist, who was not only a savior for her practical skill, but also for her empathy and her ability to put me at ease when I was really floundering.

> It's completely complementary [to Western medicine]. It doesn't interact with medications and is often used in combination with treatments, such as physiotherapy, osteopathy, and talk therapy. A common example of acupuncture and pharmaceuticals working harmoniously in my practice is the treatment of anxiety symptoms with acupuncture in those undergoing chemotherapy. The acupuncture does not interact with the chemotherapy or have any ill effects and can help the person emotionally in a huge way, which is very empowering.

With help from Hannah, we'll look at the theory, then at how it helps anxiety.

Theory

Acupuncture as part of traditional Chinese medicine (TCM) is holistic in its approach and originated at least 5,000 years ago. It is holistic in the sense that it seeks to address not only the health of the physical body, but also the mind, emotions and spirit. Hannah says:

Essentially, the goal in TCM treatment is to achieve harmony within the being and in its surroundings. When sitting with a client, our TCM diagnosis can describe a pattern of harmony or disharmony. Arriving at this diagnosis involves assessing the condition of the person's spirit, essence, energy, blood, fluids, organs, and channels.

If for example a person presents with "depression," TCM understands this as the result of deficient or stagnant energy, or the imbalance of yin and yang (the two polar opposite forces of which all things are comprised). This imbalance can present in many ways and correct, exacting diagnosis by the acupuncturist is crucial for effective timely treatment, tailor-made to that individual. The acupuncturist forms this diagnosis via an ongoing evaluation process, including tools such as looking at your posture, gait, demeanor, skin tone, brightness of eyes, voice, smell, tongue and pulse diagnosis, palpation and, of course, asking about symptoms and history.

Fundamentally, TCM believes that health is dependent on qi (energy), which, when in good health, moves in a smooth and balanced way through a chain of fourteen main channels (*jing luo*, in Chinese) mapped out throughout the body. Stress, anger, or any intense emotion acts like a traffic jam, blocking the free flow of energy in the body. For example, many people who are very stressed out complain of upper back, shoulder and neck pain.

This is because stress is causing tension in those areas, blocking the free flow of energy, causing pain and tightness, and often leading to headaches.

In accordance with TCM, along the body surface sit the acu-points—there are over 365—which can be described as wells that tap into these energy channels. With each having several functions, these points can be used in combination to correct balance and flow to achieve health. Simply put, what we are doing when we place a needle into a point is stimulating the flow of life force, bringing energy into areas of deficiency and unblocking areas of stagnation.

Acupuncture and anxiety

TCM views anxiety not simply as a brain dysfunction, but more as an inner organs dysfunction. In TCM, there exist "zang" and "fu" organs. These are not simply anatomical substances, but more importantly represent the generalization of the physiology and pathology of certain systems of the human body.

There are five "zang" and six "fu" organs. The five "zang" organs are: the heart (including the pericardium), lungs, spleen, liver and kidneys. The six "fu" organs are: the gall bladder, stomach, large intestine, small intestine, urinary bladder and the "sanjiao" (three areas of the body cavity). "Zang" and "fu" are classified by the different features of their functions. The five "zang" organs mainly manufacture and store essence: "qi," blood and body fluid.

In TCM theory, each of the "zang" organs plays a role in the emotions. Emotions and organs' health are intimately connected. "Zang" organs can develop imbalances and dysfunctions caused by dietary, environmental, lifestyle and hereditary factors.

Some example diagnoses:

Worry, dwelling or focusing too much on a particular topic, and excessive mental work are, in TCM theory, symptoms of a spleen disorder.

Lack of enthusiasm and vitality, mental restlessness, depression, insomnia and despair are symptoms of a heart disorder.

Liver disorders cause emotional symptoms, such as anger, resentment, frustration, irritability, bitterness, and "flying off the handle."

With lung disorders, we see more grief, sadness, and detachment.

With an imbalance of the kidneys, a person may be fearful, insecure, aloof, isolated, and have weak willpower.

While the heart "zang" is said to store the "shen" or spirit, in all anxiety cases the "shen" is disturbed. While a generalised anxiety disorder always affects the "shen," either primarily or secondarily, calming and harmonizing the "shen" will be the fundamental treatment.

In anxiety, Hannah explains, the most common injured organs are the spleen and heart. "When there is a disturbance in one or more of these 'zang' organs from any cause, an imbalanced emotional state can happen."

Acupuncture has also been shown in a number of studies to improve the function of the hypothalamus-pituitary-adrenal axis (HPA axis). This is basically the physical network through which stress exerts harmful effects on the body. The body secretes an assortment of hormones into the bloodstream as a reaction to stress. Researchers measured hormone levels secreted by the hypothalamus, the pituitary and the adrenal glands (HPA) involved in the fight-or-flight response.

These researchers found that: "Acupuncture blocks the chronic, stress-induced elevations of the HPA-axis hormones and the sympathetic NPY pathway."

This large and growing body of research on acupuncture's beneficial effects on various fundamental biomarkers helps to explain why it is successfully used for such a wide variety of clinical conditions.

At first I was skeptical. I would have tried anything, but acupuncture had been recommended to me several times by several people and if only for the calming down of physical symptoms, I was willing to give it a go.

In the short term, acupuncture was incredibly relaxing, but over a longer period of time, it also helped target specific physical problems, such as those aches and pains

I experienced in the morning (when my cortisol shot up), and it helped my sleeping difficulties immeasurably.

Here's why acupuncture is so good for sleep:

Sleep problems are increasingly common in modern society and often present in cases of anxiety. In TCM, sleep disorders are divided into several categories. The differentiation of these categories is crucial to correct treatment, the practitioner needs to ascertain which qi flows need to be redirected.

Some common sleep disorders often experienced as part of an anxiety condition include:

- Cannot sleep: When the spleen or liver are in disharmony, the quantity, quality and flow of blood are affected, causing sleeplessness.

- Difficulty falling asleep: This can present when "yang qi" has been blocked from yin portions of the body, preventing complete relaxation.

- Waking too early: Often associated with lifestyle issues, this is caused by poor yin energy coming from the kidneys.

- Waking in the night: This can happen when internal heat is trapped in the body. When this energy can't dissipate, insomnia occurs.

- Dream-disturbed sleep: This occurs when the mind is too active and not relaxing in sleep mode; reasons for this include "heart fire" or "liver deficiency heat."

When the practitioner has diagnosed the root cause of the disorder, the appropriate treatment will begin, balancing internal energies, calming the mind, and easing stress. While receiving acupuncture for anxiety, you will also start to experience improved sleep as a happy side effect.

Why acupuncture is worth considering for anxiety

- The term "anxiety" encompasses a large variety of symptoms and experiences that vary greatly in each sufferer. Acupuncture as a treatment for anxiety is hugely empowering as it addresses exactly what is going on for the person at that time and the treatment evolves as the condition changes and improves. At a time when a person may feel completely out of control and at the mercy of their condition, acupuncture gives back the reins and the treatment is a team effort between practitioner and patient. It treats the emotional, psychological, and physical effects with equal success without any nasty side effects, which is vital.

- It can be tailored to individuals. Acupuncture as part of TCM is holistic; it looks at the person as a whole rather than simply the condition. No two patients will receive the same treatment for the same condition. A treatment follows an extensive consultation, including questions about the patient's well-being as a whole, palpation of the pulse, and observation of the tongue.

- It has positive side-effects. Because acupuncture looks to treat the person holistically, many other aspects of the person's condition may improve. While you may present with chronic anxiety, in the course of treatment you may also notice an improvement in sleep, energy levels, circulation, and digestive function, for example.

- It looks to the root of the condition. Acupuncture is not simply focused on the presenting symptoms. Your practitioner is always looking for the root cause diagnosis. While two patients may present with a similar condition, its root causes could be completely different. By looking to the root, the fine-tuning of the treatment occurs. This means that not only will the presenting symptoms improve but, by addressing the condition from its root, it will also help to prevent a reoccurrence of this condition.

- While acupuncture is a fantastic curative medicine, it is also hugely valuable as a preventative medicine. For example, sinus conditions tend to flare up at certain times of the year for some. Rather than waiting for this to occur and seeking treatment to aid the symptoms, you can seek treatment in advance of the imminent flare-up to strengthen and balance the system to avoid the flare-up completely.

- It works for both mental and physical health. Acupuncture has been around for thousands of years and is practiced all over the world. It does not separate mental and physical health. It is recognized by both medics and patients that many physical presentations of disease have roots in mental disharmony.

Conditions like IBS, migraine, insomnia, and tension pain are often brought on or exacerbated by stress, making acupuncture a perfect treatment choice.

The second to last point here is why I make an effort to have acupuncture regularly—I'm no longer in a phase of having to deal with acute anxiety but I'd rather not feel anxious at all, so I enjoy acupuncture as a preventative measure, ensuring everything's in working order on an ongoing basis. It's also just a very relaxing experience which, in itself, is beneficial. But make sure you go to an acupuncturist who is fully qualified.[17]

And finally . . .

There are countless other treatment options out there, plenty of which are money-grabbing hoaxes, so do your homework. These few are what worked for me and, more importantly, are backed up by science—which was a big factor in my recovery.

Though not what you'd describe an "alternative" therapy, I am also a major advocate of blasting your favorite music out and dancing like your weirdest self around the kitchen. I've yet to read of any peer-reviewed studies, mind you. That and singing in the shower and the car.

If your bank balance lets you, treat yourself to regular massages. You feel like crap; treat yourself. Other than the aforementioned complementary therapies, I tried quite a bit of hypnotherapy but it just didn't do it for me, and it was very expensive. That being said, some people really love it. I think this is certainly worth doing for phobias or if you are trying to give up smoking; but for anxiety, it just didn't cut the mustard for me.

Also on the subject of things that didn't make a bloody bit of difference—I have no faith whatsoever in homeopathic medicine. I've tried it several times but never with any joy. So I just decided to stop bothering.

Give one or all of the above a try but rest assured you'll eventually find what works for you.

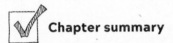 **Chapter summary**

- *Everyone should try to incorporate some form of mindfulness and meditation into their routine, but give yourself plenty of time (i.e., not just one week of mindfulness) to enjoy the benefits.*

- *Don't expect to feel anxiety-free after one session of anything*

- *There are countless alternative treatment options out there. Be discerning in your choice, be wary of anything that exploits your vulnerability.*

- *Focus on how the treatment you choose impacts your physiology. If you feel deeply relaxed for an extended period of time, this is a good thing.*

- *Alternative treatments are best approached from a "maintenance" perspective, instead of looking at them as a "cure." Find what you like and do it regularly to keep your anxiety in check.*

- *Alternative treatments are holistic and side-effect free; they can be used in tandem with more traditional treatments such as medication, if needs be.*

- *It doesn't matter if it's Reiki or knitting, as long as it makes you feel good.*

Conclusion:
What now?

AND THAT'S a wrap.

Chances are, however, this hasn't been the kind of book you read from cover to cover in one go. That's the point of it. Keep it close, and know that no matter how bad you're feeling, you'll find something in here that helps to shift it.

It's something you can dip in and out of when you need it, because getting to the point of owning your anxiety is rarely a linear experience with one destination at the end. Instead, it's—apologies, *bullsh*t-o-meters activate*—a "journey." Sorry, but it really is.

Even now, for me, though I feel I have all of the necessary tools and information at my disposal to kick anxiety's ass, and help others own it, too, I still need regular reminders of what works, which is where this book will come in handy (even for me!). I still have days where I feel less like I "own it," and more like I just "rent it."

That's okay, too. We all need reminders of our action plan; we need practical, step-by-step things to do to bring us back to a sense of balance. Even the Dalai Lama needs that. (I'm guessing, but he's human, too!) Instead of just talking about feeling like crap or wallowing in the crapness, we need positive and practical tools and techniques and, in my experience, there's no better way to face it than to first assess your situation, and then address it head on.

As I said at the outset, I would love to tell you that I have unearthed the secret to "curing" your anxiety forever more, but nobody has. And if you chase this false idea of a "cure," you'll only wind up chasing your anxious tail in circles. Instead, we need to do what's necessary—mentally and physically—so that anxiety, should it be present, can work for us rather than against us. And we look after ourselves on an ongoing basis. This is the key.

Perhaps more pertinent than during bad times, when you feel good you really have to keep doing what you're doing to maintain that wellness. You do this consistently, so that eventually, you'll prevent the fires from arising at all, rather than just putting them out as they engulf you in flames at a moment's notice.

And if you find yourself engulfed? No harm done. Each time you feel overwhelmed by a wave of anxiety, stop. Breathe. Then start by assessing your circumstances (this part helps if you do it in conversation with someone you feel you can talk to). What's going on in your life? What vulnerability factors are at play? For example, you've just had the flu, so you're below par to begin with and therefore more susceptible to negative, anxious thoughts, because your body isn't firing on all cylinders. If you are aware of what can contribute to your anxiety, it will usually make sense to you.

Now that we understand why we feel this way, we can practice self-compassion. We don't berate ourselves for feeling anxious. We give ourselves a break. We accept it. We don't run away from it. We bring ourselves back to basics. We do things that make us feel good and we opt out of things that make us feel worse. We activate our personal set of plans for addressing our symptoms of anxiety—which, for you, might be all of what's inside this book, a combination of a few elements or a whole other set of things.

When you feel bad, remember to be patient with yourself. Really working on your impatience in general will help to tame your anxiety. Stop looking for unrealistic quick-fix solutions or the one magic pill that will make it all go away. And stay the hell away from online forums where anxious people freak other anxious people out. People never write the good stuff online, only the bad. What's written is heavily weighted toward the negative and the extreme and it's not going to do you any favors. Your anxiety will settle down when you give it a chance, and know that it takes a while for hormonal imbalances to even out. Know that it's normal to feel a bit wobbly for a few days after a panic attack.

I want you to feel comforted in the knowledge that, like you, I have felt the absolute worst kind of anxiety over a long period of time, and that you can, without a shadow of a doubt, get beyond it and live your life in such a way that any abnormal levels of anxiety are rarely present at all.

Immerse yourself in information and knowledge. The most inflammatory aspect of stress and anxiety, in my opinion, is brought about by not understanding what's going on, what anxiety is, how our bodies work, how the human brain works, how the human brain has evolved and how our hormones interplay with one another. I strongly recommend that you educate yourself as much as you can. On the plus side, I think it's very interesting research, but understanding what's behind your anxiety will reduce the weight of your suffering immeasurably. In fact, it will empower you.

For those of you who are really suffering, to the point that you can't function or get through the basic aspects of your routine, know that you have lots of options.

Medication, though not for everyone, should not be viewed as a cop-out or something you should be ashamed of needing. If you need it, that's okay. I did. It's not always possible to rectify what's gone awry in your body with nothing more than good intentions. You do not need to be a hero and overcome this by merely thinking your way out of it. Anxiety is a lot more complex than that and, as you know by now, heavily wrapped up in our physiology.

You can't tell yourself to snap out of it; it takes work and it takes time. You have every right to need and ask for help, whether that's therapy, talking to a friend, discussing your options with your doctor, signing up for a mindfulness course—or all of it.

You also have a right to feel anxious or down or stressed or depressed, regardless of your life circumstances. Remember, it's not a members-only club, so don't torture yourself by the need to justify why you're feeling it.

Finally, outside of yourself, remember we have a collective responsibility to change how other people perceive mental health struggles, including anxiety. Calling bullsh*t on all of the stigmas surrounding mental health is key so that we no longer feel ashamed, embarrassed or "weak" for the fact that we all find life a little bit difficult sometimes. If we can remove the stigma, we might not feel so weighed down by it in the first place.

Taking positive action to bring yourself back to wellness and maintain it daily—that is, in my view, being a hero for yourself. It's being strong and it's being brave, even if you don't feel that way when you're having an anxious off day. The thing is, it's very easy to feel good and peaceful when things are going great and you feel physically well and the sun is shining; it's one of life's greatest skills, however, to find peace in a storm. You won't be able to and you shouldn't try to stop the rain from coming, but with the right information and the right tools—you'll weather it with ease.

In fact, you'll own it.

Important daily reminders

- *Take your diet seriously. What you put into your body matters not just in general but particularly in relation to how anxious you feel.*

- *Don't try to kid yourself about your lifestyle, you'll know if it's doing you harm.*

- *Keep doing what you're doing when you're well, not just when you feel like sh*t.*

- *Walk away from toxic relationships.*

- *Embrace your vulnerability, it's what makes you interesting.*

- *Prioritize your life: What makes you feel good goes to the top of the list and what stresses you out should be struck off.*

- *Stop apologizing or putting yourself down for your sensitive nature.*

- *Watch out for the downside of social media and social comparison.*

- *Get good at knowing the difference between your personality and your anxiety.*

- *Try CBT—either do worksheets yourself or book in for a few sessions with a CBT therapist.*

- *Prioritize activities that soothe your parasympathetic nervous system and watch out for stimulants.*

- *Help to dismantle the stigma. Spread the word. Help others.*

- *Empower yourself in the face of anxiety by educating yourself about its causes*

- *Know that anxiety can work for you rather than against you. It's not all bad.*

- *No matter how awful you feel, know that you have options and that there is a way through.*

- *Accept that stress and anxiety are part of life.*

- *Don't panic about feeling anxious after a period of time where you've felt great. Activate the* assess-and-address technique.

- *Know that by having experienced anxiety, you know yourself better. You're infinitely more in tune with yourself than anyone who's not had to do this kind of self-work. You will be stronger for it.*

- Stop trying to run away from it; instead, decide that you're going to own it.

Acknowledgments

THANK YOU TO my editor, Ciara Doorley, for giving me this rare opportunity and what I can only describe as the bloody brilliant kind of anxiety. Thanks for encouraging me every step of the way and making this an entirely enjoyable process. Thank you to the wonderful Joanna Smyth, also of Hachette, for her patience, diligence, and support.

Thank you to my agent, Faith O'Grady, for going above and beyond with your support and your genuine interest in the subject within these pages. Every assumption I had previously held about the world of book publishing was, admittedly, learned from Sandra Bullock's movie *The Proposal*. Now that I've written this, I can confirm that in reality, they're a far less scary bunch. Thank you.

Life hit a particular high when I got the call to say that my US publisher—The Experiment—were not only interested in publishing my work but were really excited about it too. Their passion and interest in continuing the important conversation around anxiety gives me all of the good feelings. Thank you to my US editor Jennifer Kurdyla for giving me this opportunity and believing in me more than I sometimes do. Thank you to Anne Marie Tomchak, Louise O'Neill, and other the other strong and inspiring women in my life who have lifted me up, particularly in relation to taking my work international.

Thank you to Dr. Malie Coyne, whose psychology expertise—in a refreshingly easy-to-understand language—underpins an enormous amount of my writing, as well as formulating all of the complementary exercises within this book. You have been such a great support and friend and I know this is the first of many things we'll do together.

Thank you also to Dr. Fionnula McHale for sharing her insights on the many physical aspects of managing anxiety and her ongoing support to me through the tough times. Thank you to Hannah O'Connell, my acupuncturist angel, who you've also heard from in this book. She just gets it, and I highly recommend all three on your journey toward wellness.

Thank you, Niall Breslin, for your encouragement and for hooking me up with all of the best people in the field of mental health and for your very kind foreword. I owe you several pints.

Thank you to my beloved friend and life mentor, Caolan Barron, who, though younger than me, is outrageously wise beyond his years. He endured many a panicked phone call from me when I had come to the conclusion that I'd definitely been possessed by an anxiety demon. Without fail, and always with humor, he'd calm me down each time, reassuring me that I was okay then, that I would be okay tomorrow, and that everything I was feeling was totally okay, too. Seriously, dude, you've had more of a positive impact on my life than you'll ever know.

Thank you for everything, Hazel and Des. Thank you to my girlfriends for being there for me when I needed them most and letting me disappear when I just needed to do that too. Thank you Una, Melanie, Laura, Aileen, the two Niamhs, Sandra, Nikki, Kevin, Sheena, Dave O., and Michael Allen. Thank you Mike Sheridan for the encouraging kick up the ass that I needed so often; I attribute a lot of my drive to your consistent guidance.

A special big fat thanks to my friend and business partner, Jo Linehan, who had my back every step of the way throughout this process. There were countless times when I'd text or call her saying, "What was I thinking, I can't write a book!" to which she'd always respond by filling me with confidence and love and support. Your presence has made my life, both personally and professionally, so wonderful. Thank you!

Thank you, Daniel, for being a proud and loving big brother who always gets in touch. Thank you to my mum and dad, Aideen and Tony, for literally picking me up off the floor when I fell to pieces and for not stopping until they'd put me back together again. I'm okay now, so we should probably resume normal family bickering, right?

Last, but by no means least, thank you to Barry, the poor, unassuming boyfriend who never expected his carefree girlfriend to have such a whopper meltdown so that she'd never want to leave her bed. Thank you for staying when things got really tough, and for reminding me every day that we're a team. Thanks for loving me just the way I am—like Bridget Jones—and for not regretting one minute of our life together. Thank you for also allowing me to watch every episode of *The Gilmore Girls*, which I know, for you, was pure torture.

Finally, thank you to *you*, dear reader, for picking up this book or recommending it to a friend. I hope it makes a difference.

Endnotes

Chapter 4

1 Rozin, Paul, and Royzman, Edward B., "Negativity bias, negativity dominance, and contagion," Department of Psychology and Solomon Asch Center for Study of Ethnopolitical Conflict, University of Pennsylvania (2001).

2 Hanson, Rick, "Confronting the Negativity Bias," rickhanson.net/how-your-brain-makes-you-easily-intimidated.

3 Adapted by Dr. Malie Coyne from mindtools.com.

Chapter 14

4 ucdavis.edu/news/mindfulness-meditation-associated-lower-stress-hormone and ncbi.nlm.nih.gov/pubmed/23527522.

5 journals.plos.org/plosone/article?id=10.1371/journal.pone.0064574.

6 blogs.scientificamerican.com/guest-blog/what-does-mindfulnessmeditation-do-to-your-brain.

Chapter 15

7 health.harvard.edu/newsletter_article/Sleep-and-mentalhealth.

8 drweil.com/healthwellness/body-mind-spirit/stressanxiety/breathing-three-exercises.

9 ncbi.nlm.nih.gov/pmc/articles/PMC3133468.

Chapter 16

10 beckinstitute.org/about-beck.

11 beckinstitute.org/faq/what-is-the-theory-behind-cognitive-behavior-therapy.

12 beckinstitute.org/frequently-asked-questions.

Chapter 20

13 havening.org/abouthavening/creators-and-developers.

14 kclpure.kcl.ac.uk/portal/en/publications/impact-of-a-singlesession-of-havening(ddf1c2e3-902b-4e70-9436-2996395b1bde)/export.html.

15 jamanetwork.com/journals/jamainternalmedicine/fullarticle/1809754.

16 richardjdavidson.com/research.

17 Cho, Z. H.; Hwang, S. C.; Wong, E. K.; Son, Y. D.; Kang, C. K.; Park, T. S.; et al. (2006). "Neural substrates, experimental evidences and functional hypothesis of acupuncture mechanisms," *Acta Neurologica Scandinavica*, 113(6): 370–77.

Resources

I've mentioned plenty of resources throughout this book, but so that you can jump to them easily, here's a handy list of the ones that I've found helpful.

Websites
- PsychologyTools.com
- GetSelfHelp.co.uk
- ALustForLife.com
- RickHanson.net
- LouiseHay.com

Downloadable CBT online worksheets
- getselfhelp.co.uk/docs/SelfHelpCourse.pdf
- Anxiety symptoms checklist worksheet:
  cci.health.wa.gov.au/~/media/CCI/Mental%20Health%20
  Professionals/Anxiety/Anxiety%20-%20Worksheets/Anxiety%20
  Worksheet%20-%2001%20-%20Anxiety%20Symptoms%20
  Worksheet.pdf
- Postpone your worry worksheet:
  cci.health.wa.gov.au/Resources/Looking-After-Yourself/
  Worry-and-Rumination
- Accepting uncertainty worksheet:
  cci.health.wa.gov.au/~/media/CCI/Consumer%20Modules/
  What%20Me%20Worry/What%20Me%20Worry%20-%2009%20-%20
  Accepting%20Uncertainty.pdf
- Simple thought record worksheet:
  psychologytools.com/worksheet/
  simple-thought-challenging-record

Apps
- Calm
- Headspace
- Stop, Breathe & Think

Books

Anything by Elizabeth Gilbert, Brené Brown, or Cheryl Strayed

Breslin, Niall, *Me and My Mate Jeffrey* (Dublin: Hachette Books Ireland) 2015.

Brown, Brené, *Rising Strong* (New York: Penguin Random House) 2017.

Davis, Martha, *The Relaxation and Stress Reduction Workbook Volume 6* (Oakland: New Harbinger Publications) 2008.

Gaffney, Maureen, *Flourishing* (London: Penguin UK) 2016.

Gilbert, Elizabeth, *Eat Pray Love* (New York: Riverhead Books) 2007.

Greenberger, Dennis and Padesky, Christine A., *Mind over Mood,* 2nd ed. (New York: Guilford Press) 2016.

Hanson, Rick, *Buddha's Brain: The Practical Neuroscience of Happiness, Love and Wisdom* (Oakland: New Harbinger Publications) 2009.

Huffington, Arianna, *Thrive* (New York: Penguin Random House) 2015.

Jeffers, S., *Feel the Fear and Do It Anyway* (New York: Ballantine Books) 2006.

Kahneman, Daniel, *Thinking, Fast and Slow* (New York: Farrar, Straus and Giroux) 2013.

Kennerley, Helen, *Overcoming Anxiety* (London: Robinson) 2014.

Knight, Sarah, *The Life-Changing Magic of Not Giving a F**k* (New York: Little, Brown and Company) 2015.

Kondo, Marie, *The Life-Changing Magic of Tidying Up* (New York: Ten Speed Press) 2014.

Shapiro, Deb, *Your Body Speaks Your Mind* (Boulder, CO: Sounds True) 2006.

Strayed, Cheryl, *Wild* (New York: Alfred A. Knopf) 2012.

Strayed, Cheryl, *Tiny Beautiful Things* (New York: Vintage Books) 2012.

Templar, Richard, *The Rules of Life*, 4th ed. (London: Pearson Educational) 2015.

Tolle, Eckhart, *The Power of Now* (Vancouver, Canada: Namaste Publishing) 2004.

Williams, C., *Overcoming Anxiety, Stress and Panic* (Boca Raton, FL: CRC Press [Taylor & Francis]) 2012.

Text permissions

About the author

CAROLINE FORAN is a freelance lifestyle journalist and cofounder of the digital publishing venture GAFFInteriors.ie.

Prior to her career in media, she obtained a degree in communications and a master's in film and TV, both from Dublin City University.

Caroline lives in Dublin. She is the author of *Own It*. and *The Confidence Kit*.